DECISIVE TREATISE

◆

EPISTLE DEDICATORY

Averroës

THE BOOK OF THE

Decisive Treatise

DETERMINING THE CONNECTION

BETWEEN THE LAW AND WISDOM

&

Epistle Dedicatory

كتاب فصل المقال
وتقرير ما بين الشريعة والحكمة من الاتصال

رسالة الإهداء
الملقبة بالضميمة

Translation, with introduction and notes, by
Charles E. Butterworth

Brigham Young University Press ◆ *Provo, Utah* ◆ *2008*

LIBRARY OF CONGRESS CATALOGING-IN-PUBLICATION DATA

Averroës, 1126–1198.
  [Faṣl al-maqāl fī mā bayna al-sharīᶜah wa-al-ḥikmah min al-ittiṣāl.
English & Arabic]
  The book of the decisive treatise determining the connection
between the law and wisdom ; and, The epistle dedicatory / Averroes ;
translation, with introduction and notes, by Charles E. Butterworth.
    p.   cm.— (Islamic translation series)
  1. Islam and philosophy—Early works to 1800. I. Title: Book of
the decisive treatise determining the connection between the law and
wisdom ; and, The epistle dedicatory. II. Averroës, 1126–1198. Faṣl
al-maqāl fī mā bayna al-sharīᶜah wa-al-ḥikmah min al-ittiṣāl. Ḍamīmah.
English & Arabic. III. Title: Epistle dedicatory. IV. Title. V. Series.
  B749.F32 E5   2001
  181'.92—dc21   00-012879
                                                                CIP

ISBN 978-0-8425-2479-7

PRINTED IN THE UNITED STATES OF AMERICA

FOR BEATRICE

a model of courage, compassion, and wisdom

Contents

The Book of the Decisive Treatise

Epistle Dedicatory

◆　◆　◆

Foreword to the Series

The Islamic Translation Series: Philosophy, Theology, and Mysticism (hereafter ITS) is designed not only to further scholarship in Islamic studies but, by encouraging the translation of Islamic texts into the technical language of contemporary Western scholarship, to assist in the integration of Islamic studies into Western academia and to promote global perspectives in the disciplines to which it is devoted. If this goal is achieved, it will not be for the first time: Historians well know that, during the so-called Middle Ages, a portion of the philosophical, scientific, and mathematical wealth of the Islamic tradition entered into and greatly enriched the West. Even Christian theology was affected, as is brilliantly evidenced in the works of St. Thomas Aquinas and other scholastics.

Manuscripts submitted to ITS for consideration are, of course, evaluated without regard to the religious, methodological, or political preferences of the translators or to their gender or national origins. The translator of each text, not the editors of the series nor the members of the advisory board, is solely responsible for the volume in question.

On behalf of Daniel C. Peterson, the executive editor, and members of the advisory board, I wish to express deep appreciation to the cosponsoring institutions—the Institute for the Study and Preservation of Ancient Religious Texts at Brigham Young University and the Foundation for Interreligious Diplomacy (and its director, Charles Randall Paul)—for their gracious support of this project.

—PARVIZ MOREWEDGE
Editor in Chief
Rutgers, The State University of New Jersey

◆ ◆ ◆

Brigham Young University and its Institute for the Study and Preservation of Ancient Religious Texts are pleased to sponsor and publish the Islamic Translation Series: Philosophy, Theology, and Mysticism (ITS). We wish to express our appreciation to the editor in chief of ITS, Parviz Morewedge, for joining us in this important project. We are especially grateful to James L. and Beverley Sorenson of Salt Lake City for their generous support, which made ITS possible, and to the Ashton Family Foundation of Orem, Utah, which kindly provided additional funding so that we might continue.

Islamic civilization represents nearly fourteen centuries of intense intellectual activity, and believers in Islam number in the hundreds of millions. The texts that will appear in ITS are among the treasures of this great culture. But they are more than that. They are properly the inheritance of all the peoples of the world. As an institution of The Church of Jesus Christ of Latter-day Saints, Brigham Young University is honored to assist in making these texts available to many for the first time. In doing so, we hope to serve our fellow human beings, of all creeds and cultures. We also follow the admonition of our own tradition, to "seek . . . out of the best books words of wisdom," believing, indeed, that "the glory of God is intelligence."

—DANIEL C. PETERSON
Executive Editor
Brigham Young University

◆ ◆ ◆

A NOTE ON SPELLING

In this work, terms of Arabic derivation found in *Webster's Third New International Dictionary* generally follow the first spelling given therein and are treated as regular English words. Otherwise, Arabic or Persian words and proper names have been transliterated following, with few exceptions, the standard recommended by the *International Journal of Middle East Studies*.

Preface

The goal of the translation set forth here is to present Averroës' Arabic text in as faithful a manner as is consonant with readable English. To this end, key terms have always been translated in the same way, unless otherwise noted, and great effort has been expended to preserve the legal style of the treatise. Sometimes it has been necessary to make precise antecedents that Averroës leaves imprecise, just as upon occasion it was appropriate to ease the reader over difficult passages by introducing explanatory links in square brackets. All such interpolations are my own. Though aware that any translation is necessarily an interpretation of sorts, I have made every effort to let the voice of authority here be that of Averroës and thus to avoid the temptation of letting my understanding of the text speak more loudly than the text itself. A more readable translation can always be achieved by recasting the text to reflect the translator's sense of what goes best in English. That procedure tends, however, to purchase readability at the price of fidelity to nuances within the original text.

The translation is based on Muhsin Mahdi's revised version of the Arabic text, *Kitāb faṣl al-maqāl*, edited by George F. Hourani (Leiden: E. J. Brill, 1959). The revisions were made on the basis of a re-examination of the manuscripts used by Hourani and the readings originally chosen by him. Section numbers have been added by me, as have all other textual divisions and punctuation. In the Arabic text, the page references in square brackets refer to the pages of Marcus Joseph Müller's original Arabic edition, *Philosophie und Theologie von Averroes* (Munich: n.p., 1859). An earlier version of the introduction appeared in *Arabic Sciences and Philosophy* 5, no. 1 (March, 1995): 93–119, under the title "The Source That Nourishes: Averroes's Decisive Determination."

To scores of students who have struggled over various versions of this translation for the last decade and longer, it is a pleasure to offer an expression of deep gratitude. Special thanks are due also to Thomas

Pangle for a careful, critical reading of the translation—above all, for his persistent querying about antecedents. But here, as in so many other matters, supreme acknowledgment for help and encouragement is due Muhsin S. Mahdi. It was he who first suggested I undertake such a task and who made important suggestions for improvement at many stages of the endeavor. I only hope the finished product somehow reflects the gracious assistance of so many thoughtful readers.

—CHARLES E. BUTTERWORTH
Washington, D.C.
December, 1998

Biographical Sketch
of Averroës (1126–1198)

Thanks to Saint Thomas Aquinas and Dante, Abū al-Walīd Muḥammad ibn Aḥmad ibn Muḥammad ibn Rushd—or Averroës, as he is more commonly called in the West—is well known as *the* commentator on Aristotle. Much as he deserves that appellation, he must also be recognized as an accomplished commentator on Plato, a physician, a practicing judge, a jurist, and a spokesman for political and religious problems of his day—the latter addressed in independent treatises and commentaries of sorts on Abū Ḥāmid al-Ghazālī (1058–1111), whose attacks on the philosophers are examined in the work by Averroës presented here.

We learn of Averroës' life from a few personal references scattered throughout his writings, from traditional Arabic biographies, and from two famous histories of the Maghreb: one written by Aḥmad ibn Muḥammad al-Makkarī and the other by ʿAbd al-Wāḥid al-Marrakushī. In the biographies and in these two histories, Averroës' intellectual acumen and profound accomplishments in jurisprudence, medicine, poetry, philosophy, natural science, and theology are praised extravagantly. The autobiographical references we do encounter in Averroës' writings serve mainly to explain the imperfect character of the work being offered to the public, but show thereby how busily engaged he was in other activities.

He was born in Córdoba, the son and grandson of noted judges, or qadis, his grandfather having served as the chief qadi of Córdoba and of Andalusia. During the first two decades of Averroës' life, the ruling Almoravid dynasty was so wracked by internal dissension that it fell to the emergent Almohad forces, under the famous warrior ʿAbd al Muʾmin. The sources describe this as a period of study for Averroës—one in which he devoted himself to jurisprudence, medicine, theology, and the natural sciences. Indeed, his desire for learning is said to have been so intense that he relaxed from his philosophical studies by passing to the reading of poetry or history. Two biographers even go so far as to claim that this attachment to learning was so intense and played so dominant a role in the way he organized his time that he studied all but two nights of his life—his wedding night and the night his father died.

Though he was known as much for his practical activity as a qadi and advisor to rulers as for his theoretical accomplishments, we hear nothing of Averroës' political activity until he was nearly thirty years of age. Called to Marrakesh in 1153 by ʿAbd al-Muʾmin, by then ruler of the Almohad dynasty, Averroës was named advisor to ʿAbd al-Muʾmin's grandiose project of building schools and literary institutions throughout the realm. Some sixteen years later, he was appointed qadi of Seville and held the post until called to Marrakesh in 1182 as personal physician to ʿAbd al-Muʾmin's successor, Abū Yaʿqūb.[1] The treatise *On the Substance of the Celestial Sphere,* dated in 1178 from Marrakesh, and references in the *Meteorologica* to earthquakes occurring in Córdoba show that Averroës traveled extensively during these years. The historians praise Abū Yaʿqūb highly as an exceedingly handsome, courteous, intelligent, and well-educated man. He is said to have loved science and to have studied medicine as well as philosophy. Indeed, one account of the first meeting between this exceptionally gifted ruler and his extraordinarily promising subject emphasizes the ruler's philosophic learning: when Ibn Ṭufayl presented Averroës to Abū Yaʿqūb, the sovereign asked Averroës his opinion about whether the world was created or had existed eternally, a question with far-reaching theological implications; and noting Averroës' confusion about a suitable reply, Abu Yaʿqūb turned to Ibn Ṭufayl to pursue the question and displayed such a mastery of the teachings of the philosophers about the problem as to reassure Averroës that the question was entirely sincere.

Averroës was named personal physician to Abū Yaʿqūb but served in that capacity only a matter of months before being appointed qadi of Córdoba. Abū Yaʿqūb, killed two years later (that is, in 1184) during the siege of Santarem, was succeeded by his son Yaʿqūb ibn Yūsuf (later to be known as Abū Yūsuf Yaʿqūb)—a ruler praised as a great warrior and builder. Averroës had a very close relationship with the new ruler— almost one of intimate friendship—but was nonetheless punished in 1195, along with other notable scholars, for being overly occupied with philosophy and "the sciences of the Ancients." It is not clear what prompted the philosophically minded Abū Yūsuf to visit a punishment of this sort upon his friend and close advisor. Some claim that he wished to rebuke Averroës for an act of insolence, others that he was seeking to placate zealous partisans of religion within the court. Averroës' punishment consisted in his being banished to Lucena, a small town near Córdoba. The banishment lasted only two years; shortly after having returned to the court in Marrakesh, Averroës died.

By the age of thirty—that is, not long after he was first called to the court in Marrakesh—Averroës had already composed some treatises on logic. Then, subsequent to having been presented to Abū Yaᶜqūb in 1168 as the one most qualified to undertake the task of commenting on Aristotle's works, he began the work for which he is so noted. For the next dozen or so years—that is, from about 1169 to 1182—Averroës composed middle commentaries on all of Aristotle's logical works, including the *Rhetoric* and the *Poetics;* on most of the major works having to do with physical science (namely, the *Physics, On the Heavens, On Generation and Corruption, Meteorologica,* and *On the Soul*); on the *Metaphysics;* and on the *Nicomachean Ethics.* Moreover, he wrote short commentaries or summaries on some of Aristotle's other works in natural science (that is, on the *Parts of Animals, Generation of Animals,* and *Parva Naturalia*) as well as two treatises (*On the Application of the Intellect and Intelligibles* and *On the Substance of the Celestial Sphere*). And Averroës also composed a large commentary on Aristotle's *Posterior Analytics.* In addition to these writings related to Aristotle and Aristotelian investigations, Averroës composed treatises on topics of more immediate concern to fellow Muslims. Among these are the two works presented here—the *Decisive Treatise,* with its *Epistle Dedicatory*—and the sequel to them, *Kashf ᶜan manāhij al-adilla fī ᶜaqāᵓid al-milla* (Uncovering the methods of proofs with respect to the beliefs of the religious community), plus the famous refutation of al-Ghazālī, the *Tahāfut al-Tahāfut* (Incoherence of the Incoherence).

In the next dozen or so years—that is, from the beginning of the reign of Abū Yūsuf Yaᶜqūb until about the time he was banished in 1195—Averroës composed large commentaries on Aristotle's *Physics, On the Heavens, On the Soul,* and *Metaphysics;* a middle commentary on Galen's *On Fevers;* a short or middle commentary on Plato's *Republic;* a middle commentary on al-Ghazālī's famous work about the foundations of jurisprudence known as *Al-Mustaṣfā* (The Sufficiency), which he entitled *Al-Ḍarurī fī uṣūl al-fīqh aw mukhtaṣar al-Mustaṣfā* (The Necessary with respect to the fundamentals of jurisprudence, or the summary of the Sufficiency); and a small book entitled *On the Happiness of the Soul.* Moreover, he composed a substantial work on jurisprudence, the *Bidāyat al-mujtahid wa nihāyat al-muqtaṣid* (The legal interpreter's beginning and the mediator's ending).

In all of his writings, Averroës shows his distinctive style—one that is direct and forceful and quite unlike that of either of the philosophers whose defense he undertakes in the work before us. Like both of them, he pursues questions tenaciously. Unlike Avicenna, however, he is little given to whimsical comparisons between religion and philosophy. Though as concerned as Avicenna about the relationship between revelation and reason or prophecy and prudence, he is deeply apprehensive about facile similarities that might lead to confusion. He is nowhere as imaginative or even as speculative as the great second teacher, al-Fārābī (second, that is, after Aristotle), but seems to share more with him in understanding and in approach. Like al-Fārābī, for example, he was persuaded that science, and with it philosophy, had been completed by Aristotle but that it still needed to be recovered and, above all, protected in each age. These are the goals to which Averroës addresses himself in all of his works: the commentaries on Aristotle and Plato are intended to recover or rediscover the ancient teaching and explain it to those who can profit from it; the public writings—that is, those written to address issues of the day—seek to preserve the possibility of philosophical pursuits in an increasingly hostile religious environment. For Averroës, philosophy is ever the friend of religion; it seeks to discover the same truth as religion and to bring the learned to respect divine revelation. He explains this best, perhaps, in his *Middle Commentary on the* Parva naturalia (Second Treatise, chapter 3) when, talking about prophecy and divinely inspired perceptions, he notes that

> the discussion of these matters, though exceedingly difficult for human perception, must nevertheless reach the utmost limit the nature of human perception permits; for this, and nothing else, is the substance of happiness.

Translator's Introduction
to the *Decisive Treatise*

I. Preliminary considerations

A quarter of a century ago, a scholar embarking on a study of Machiavelli lamented, not entirely in jest, the absence of any terrain not already marked out, as though in neon lights, by an illustrious predecessor who had written the definitive study on Machiavelli nearly a score of years prior.[1] Two ground-breaking studies by Muhsin Mahdi, dating back seventeen and thirty-seven years respectively,[2] place the erstwhile student of Averroës' *Kitāb faṣl al-maqāl* (Book of the decisive treatise) and the so-called *Ḍamīma* (now properly known as the *Epistle Dedicatory,* or *Epistle on Divine Knowledge*) in a not entirely dissimilar dilemma. Indeed, Mahdi has clearly proven that the *Ḍamīma* and the *Faṣl al-maqāl* are, respectively, the first and second works of a trilogy and has masterfully identified the major question in both. Nor are Mahdi's contributions the only ones that chart out the contours of these works, especially the *Decisive Treatise.* To his two studies must be added more than a dozen others composed by almost as many scholars since the beginning of the twentieth century, most written in conjunction with a translation of the *Decisive Treatise* or of it as well as of the *Epistle Dedicatory.*[3]

Only two considerations justify yet another attempt to explain the *Decisive Treatise* and encourage anyone foolhardy enough to undertake it. First, Mahdi's study focuses solely on what he considers to be the beginning half of the work. Second, many of the reflections prompting my new English translation of the *Decisive Treatise,* as elaborated in this interpretative essay, promise to benefit those who seek to understand its mysteries.

Of this extensive list of studies, Mahdi's essay on the *Decisive Treatise* and Hourani's introduction to his English translation of that work demand

immediate attention, not least because of the different way they understand the structure of the text. Whereas Hourani divides it into an introduction (§1 [1.1–9])[4] plus three chapters (§§2–11 [1.10–7.6], §§12–37
[7.7–18.19], and §§38–60 [18.19–26.14]), Mahdi thinks it consists of an
introduction (§1 [1.1–9]) and two major parts (§§2–37 [1.10–18.19] and
§§38–60 [18.19–26.14]). Hourani, in agreement with Mahdi as concerns
the introduction and final chapter or part, differs both insofar as he
divides the first part into two chapters and by where he suggests placing
the break between his chapter one and chapter two. Although my understanding of the way this text is structured calls for more than Mahdi's two
parts or Hourani's three chapters, I can discern no reason for the break
urged by the latter. It ignores not only the sense of the argument but also
Averroës' peculiar style in this treatise.

After having shown why philosophy is obligatory according to the
divine Law (§2 [1.10–2.8]), Averroës enters upon a long series of arguments to show why one can follow that stricture only if the study of syllogistic reasoning is also embraced (§§3–10 [2.9–6.14]). Having made
that point, he embarks upon another task—one that seems to occupy his
attention in one way or another throughout the rest of the treatise but
certainly through that portion of it running from this point on to the formal summary and apology that Hourani and Mahdi take as ending the
next section of the text—that is, chapter two and part one respectively
(§37 [18.14–19]). Averroës signals that he is about to engage upon this
new task by formally declaring, "Since all of this has been determined"
(wa idhā taqarrara hādhā kulluhu), and speaking for the first time of the
beliefs of the Muslim community as well as of the various natures of
human beings. The discussion of consensus *(ijmāʾ)* that comes up in the
immediate sequel is intimately linked with the idea of Muslim commu-
nal life. In other words, none of this is in keeping with a summary statement intended to close an argument.

Still, Hourani's introduction is thoroughly helpful, not least because
it so skillfully defines the intellectual context surrounding the subject of
the treatise and provides such a fine overview of the broader themes
treated here. In the course of focusing primarily on what he terms part
one of the treatise, Mahdi shows why it is to be identified as concerned
with what can be inferred from the divine Law. Paying special attention
to Averroës' use of such stylistic devices as *taqrīr*—that is, the "determining" or "determination" of the treatise's title—and its derivatives, as
well as to the terms *idhā* and *in* used to begin syllogisms, he divides this
first part into five sections and seventeen subsections. As the title of his

essay intimates, Mahdi proposes no grand explanation; instead, he limits
himself to comments and reflections on these stylistic devices as a means
of pointing to some of the questions Averroës raises in the first part of
the *Decisive Treatise*.[5]

II. The *Decisive Treatise:* Its title and dramatic setting

A. The title

This work, identified in the Escorial manuscript as *Kitāb faṣl al-maqāl wa
taqrīr mā bayn al-sharīʿa wa al-ḥikma min al-ittiṣāl* (The book of the decisive
treatise, determining the connection between the Law and wisdom), has
been referred to in various other ways by the biographers.[6] Most important,
though, is that none of them calls it a "book" *(kitāb)*. Nor does Averroës
himself ever refer to it by this name. In its sequel, the *Kitāb al-kashf ʿan
manāhij al-adilla*, he calls it a "speech" *(qawl)* while designating as a "book"
only the *Kashf* itself (see 27.10, 16). Yet, because he also uses the term
"speech" in the *Decisive Treatise* to identify the *Epistle Dedicatory*, or *Ḍamīma*
(§17 [11.6]), doubt remains as to the precise character of this work.

Important as they are, the terms "Law" and "wisdom" may be passed
over now with the single aside that *sharīʿa* and *sharʿ* are both referred to
here as Law (the uppercase letter serving to denote their special status
as revealed law), for these terms receive ample attention in the sequel.
The term *faṣl* literally means "separating" but also has a legal significance and can thus suggest something like "decisive [rendering of] judgment." *Taqrīr* is also a legal term, one denoting a decision set down by a
judge, or an assignment or stipulation. As Muhsin Mahdi has cogently
observed, it and its derivatives seem to constitute organizing principles
by means of which Averroës indicates the steps of his argument. The
most literal, and perhaps most accurate, rendering of the title would
thus be "Book of decisively judging the statement and determining the
connection between the Law and wisdom." Too unwieldy for normal pur-
poses, it nonetheless draws attention to the fundamental question of
what is to be decisively judged, as well as to the way that judgment is jux-
taposed to the connection Averroës is intent upon determining as concerns the Law and wisdom.

B. The dramatic setting

Book or speech, the *Decisive Treatise* is characterized above all by the
legal context in which Averroës couches his whole exposition as well as

by his repeated references to, and even attacks upon, the jurists and dialectical theologians. His abundant recourse to Qurʾānic verses and to language highly evocative of the Muslim revelation amply indicates that he seeks to present this argument as something like a plea before a tribunal in which the divine Law of Islam is the sole authority. He speaks, for example, of the faithful person *(muʾmin)* and of faith *(īmān)*, rather than of someone who merely holds a belief or of belief. And to show more clearly how closely linked are philosophy and the Law, he both distinguishes between and subtly confuses the verbs *ʿarafa* (to be cognizant of) and *ʿalima* (to know) so that the person who is cognizant of God—a perfectly respectable idea to any member of the faith—sometimes seems to be the same as someone who knows Him. Similarly, Averroës reminds the reader again and again of the way Islam has developed over time, of the beliefs shared by the members of the Muslim community, of the allegiance all feel to "this divine Law of ours," of its truth, of the responsibility placed upon a Muslim as Muslim, and of the intention of the Law as well as of the Lawgiver. Averroës provides, moreover, immediate evidence that he intends here to respect the strictures of the Muslim community. In the opening sentence he trumpets clearly that the investigative goal he will pursue is limited to "the perspective of Law-based reflection."

Still, his goal is to determine the connection between this Law and wisdom, or philosophy. Even though he defends or explains the latter in terms set by the former, he does not thereby concede its subservience. If anything, he tries to avoid juxtaposing the two in such a hierarchical fashion. Neither priority nor ascendance is at issue; the connection to be determined eventually is close to one of parity—that is, agreement on all levels.

III. The structure of the argument

Generally speaking, Mahdi's suggestion that the treatise consists of two parts is sound. I would add, however, that each is further divided into two additional subparts and that each of the larger parts is perfectly balanced with the other. The first proceeds explicitly according to what the perspective of Law-based reflection requires (a stipulation that remains in effect, but is interpreted more broadly in the second part). It is preceded by an introduction (§1 [1.1–9]) and followed by a summary (§37 [18.14–19]), much the same way as the second major part is preceded by the summary in question and followed by a conclusion (§§59–60 [25.20–26.14]). In my division of the text, then, the introduction, summary, and conclusion are also counted as subparts. The first and larger part consists of two basic subparts: the first of these urges the obligation, according to the divine Law, to study philosophy and logic (§§2–10 [1.10–6.14]); the second seeks to confirm that argument by showing that anything proved by demonstration necessarily accords with the divine Law (§§11–36 [6.14–18.14]). This is followed by a summary statement that brings this first series of reflections to an end and offers an apology for discussing such matters in an otherwise public writing.

But the treatise does not end on that note. After the summary statement, there is a second part. It, too, consists of two basic subparts. The first examines, albeit not for the first time, the intention of the Law and the methods used in it for speaking to all the people,[7] thus permitting Averroës to emphasize what was discovered in the preceding two series of arguments (§§38–51 [18.19–23.18]). The second then goes on to explain how ignorance of these methods has caused factions to arise within Islam, the idea being that they need not have arisen. Indeed, if Averroës' explanation were followed, there would be no factions (§§52–58 [23.19–25.19]).

Following the introduction, then, in the next two subparts of the treatise, Averroës draws a series of inferences from the Law to show why the study of philosophy and logic is needful and pursues different attempts to defend the teachings of the philosophers from misguided attacks by al-Ghazālī and other confused dialectical theologians. After a formal summary to explain what he has done and apologize for breaking his own strictures about the proper setting for this kind of discussion, Averroës turns to a consideration of the intention of the Law and the Lawgiver, as well as of the way the philosophers—but not the dialectical theologians or the jurists—respect that intention and strive to protect it. These reflections, set forth in the fifth subpart, are followed in the next by an inquiry into how the harm he has been combating arose in the first place and then by a formal concluding subpart.[8]

So stated, this understanding of the work's structure differs mainly in emphasis from the one sketched out by Mahdi and varies only slightly from that proposed by Hourani. As has already been noted, there is a break in the argument that corresponds with what Hourani identifies as chapter one. But, as has also been explained, that break actually occurs earlier than he indicates. Hourani does not speak at greater length about the structure of the work, preferring instead to concentrate on the arguments and their antecedents. And Mahdi's desire to show how Averroës' inferences from the Law allow him to advance his argument, coupled with his conviction that they are signaled in the stylistic devices he takes to constitute sections and subsections, keeps him from dwelling much on the formal structure of the treatise.

A. Introduction
(§1 [1.1–9])

At no point in this treatise is the primacy of the Law at question. The extent to which it provides the framework for all that follows is best exemplified, as has been noted, by Averroës' opening statement that his goal is "to investigate, from the perspective of Law-based reflection." What he proposes to investigate is a single thing, albeit one that has two subjects: "Whether reflection upon philosophy and the sciences of logic is permitted, prohibited, or commanded—and this as a recommendation or as an obligation—by the Law." In other words, the ensuing investigation is designed to put philosophical and logical reflection into a particular legal category.

That task is accomplished almost immediately. Averroës then goes beyond this stated goal, both to defend what he has done and to expand upon it. In keeping with these new endeavors, he is prompted to speak of the "connection" *(ittiṣāl)* referred to in the title of the *Decisive Treatise,* and thus of the Law's intention. There is no need at this juncture for him to speak of philosophy's intent, that having been done in the opening paragraphs. Yet, in speaking of the connection and of the Law's intention, Averroës does manage to exculpate philosophers generally—but especially his two famous predecessors within the Islamic tradition, al-Fārābī and Avicenna (Ibn Sīnā)—from charges of unbelief leveled against them.

B. Philosophy and logic are obligatory
(§§2–10 [1.10–6.14])

1. Averroës seeks first to prove that it is obligatory to reflect upon philosophy, then turns to the question of logic. His argument for the first is quite straightforward but somewhat truncated. Identifying philosophy as inquiry into the existent things *(al-mawjūdāt)* rather than into being *(mawjūd)* simply, he further claims that its goal is "consideration of them insofar as they are an indication of the Artisan." Still, the first part of this definition is consonant with the traditional understanding of philosophy as an art that seeks to know what being is and how it comes about, in the sense that the general entity can be known only through its particular instances. The second part of the definition is more problematic; but by recourse to Qurʾānic citations for its verification, Averroës places it beyond question.

The syllogism used to prove that the Law commands philosophy is not sound, even when rephrased:

(1) Philosophy is investigation of divine order.
(2) Investigation of divine order is commanded by the Law.
Ergo, philosophy is commanded by the Law.

As has been noted, the first premise is not evident; and the second stretches the Qurʾānic verses cited as evidence. Yet, no friend of philosophy would contest the syllogism's conclusion, namely, that philosophy falls within the category of what is "commanded" *(maʾmūr)* by the Law. Nor would friends of religion query Averroës' use of Qurʾānic verses to show that it is "obligatory."

2. Undeterred by the weakness of the syllogism and the proofs cited in its defense, Averroës moves to the next phase of the argument and affirms, "since it has been determined that the Law makes it obligatory to reflect upon existing things by means of the intellect, and to consider them" (§3 [2.9]), such reflection must be carried out by syllogistic reasoning. The syllogistic reasoning at issue is the best kind: demonstration. To reach this conclusion, Averroës determines the obligation to reflect and consider, affirms that consideration means inferring, concludes provisionally that this is syllogistic reasoning, restates that conclusion but qualifies the syllogistic reasoning as intellectual and notes that it is obligatory, and then extends it to embrace demonstration. Differently stated, for Averroës, consideration can refer to nothing but syllogistic reasoning— and demonstrative syllogistic reasoning at that.

Important as are the advances made thus far, Averroës must still assuage the doubts of his fellow Muslims, especially those concerned with the science of jurisprudence and the syllogistic reasoning used in it. This he undertakes in the immediate sequel (§4 [2.13–3.12]) and then, in the rest of this subpart (§§5–10 [3.13–6.14]), sets about proving the need to have recourse to the books of distinguished predecessors, even if they are not Muslims. He uses three different kinds of arguments to reassure his fellow Muslims: a summary of the preceding arguments to emphasize that it is obligatory to study logic [2.13–3.1], an inference from the similarity of purpose between the jurist and the philosopher [3.2–7], and a reply to the putative objection that syllogistic reasoning of this sort is heretical innovation [3.8–12].[9]

The fundamental premise of the first argument—a summary of the conclusions reached in the preceding two sections, "since the Law has urged cognizance of God (may He be exalted) and of all of the things existing through Him by means of demonstration"—depends so much upon them, and upon a series of additional premises never more than dialectical in character, that Averroës indirectly attenuates the conclusion. Instead of declaring, "Therefore, it bcomes obligatory" *(fa-yajib)*, he inserts the qualifier *qad* and merely suggests, "Therefore, it perhaps becomes obligatory" (§4 [2.20]).[10] Troublesome as it appears here, this softening also prepares for that aspect of the subsequent argument which emphasizes the need for most people to take the Law in its apparent sense— that is, not to use sophisticated tools of reasoning to understand it. Now, however, Averroës dwells on this ancillary characteristic of logic and presents it as merely a tool for aiding reflection.

On the one hand, intellectual syllogistic reasoning is as permissible to the one who discerns that "the Law has urged cognizance of God" as it is to the jurist who obeys "the command to obtain juridical understanding of the statutes" and infers from it "the obligation to become cognizant of the kinds of juridical syllogistic reasoning, and which of them is syllogistic reasoning and which not" [3.2–3]. And, on the other hand, intellectual syllogistic reasoning is even more permissible or praiseworthy than juridical reasoning. After all, no one would deny that the task of gaining cognizance of God is more laudable than that of obtaining "juridical understanding of the statutes."[11]

This parallel between juridical syllogistic reasoning and intellectual syllogistic reasoning can be used to blunt any charge that the latter constitutes some kind of heretical innovation. The same considerations that permitted Muslims to develop the former hold for the latter—especially given the greater worth of the latter. Here, though, almost like a lawyer eager to use every last scrap of evidence, Averroës adduces yet another argument. He begins by presupposing that what is accepted by most Muslims is sound, for he notes simply that only "a small group of strict literalists" reject intellectual syllogistic reasoning. Then he turns to unimpeachable authority to conclude that "they are refuted by the texts" of the Qur'ān.[12]

Now, then, the question arises as to how one might learn about intellectual syllogistic reasoning. Noting the immensity of the endeavor, Averroës proposes making use of anyone who has already gained some knowledge of this tool and doing so "whether that other person shares our religion or not" (§6 [3.20–21]). There is nothing objectionable about such a procedure. Indeed, had he wished, Averroës might have enlisted the testimony of so illustrious a predecessor as al-Kindī to buttress this argument.[13] Eschewing the rhetorical ploy so readily available, he asserts instead—and this without any attempt at defense—that "all that is needed with respect to reflection about the matter of intellectual syllogistic reasonings has been investigated by the Ancients in the most complete manner" (§7 [4.3–4]).

Averroës makes this proposal, it seems, in order to facilitate the next step of the argument—namely, moving from the acquisition of the tools for reasoning to the content of such reasoning. Precisely those considerations that warranted turning to the books of the Ancients for the tools, regardless of their religious beliefs and practices, hold when it is a question of putting those tools to their proper use—that is, to "consider existing things and the indication of artfulness in them." Once again, the importance of the endeavor makes it seem all the more justifiable: "For one who is not cognizant of the artfulness is not cognizant of what has been artfully made, and one who is not cognizant of what has been artfully made is not cognizant of the Artisan" (§8 [4.7–9]). Only the tentativeness of the conclusion he draws ("therefore, it is perhaps obligatory") bears witness to the enormity of this logical jump. And he repeats it in the section immediately following (§9 [5.7–8]).[14]

Such tentativeness is necessary insofar as the arguments set forth thus far are by no means without flaw, but also—and surely more significantly—because they address only the most learned, whereas the Law calls to all. This disparity comes to light with Averroës' attempt, in the immediate sequel, to equate the "aim and intention" in the books of the Ancients with "the very intention to which the Law urges us" (§10 [5.13]). Both the disparity and the question of the Law's intention—or the relationship between the disparity and the Law's intention—will occupy Averroës in the rest of the treatise. He understands the Law to be addressed to all people, but in different ways; there is reason to wonder whether the jurists and dialectical theologians whose writings he will examine hereafter have such an understanding.

Before turning to those questions, however, Averroës responds to yet another possible criticism of the philosophy and logic set forth in the books of the Ancients. He seeks, as though reinforcing his earlier claim that they are sound instruments, to show that they are not somehow harmful in and of themselves. Given the obnoxious conclusions reached by some predecessors who used these instruments, not to mention fellow Muslims who have gone astray after recourse to them, one might wonder how innocuous such instruments really are. Averroës insists that such errancy is merely an accidental effect but nonetheless posits two conditions that anyone who would use them must fulfill. The first, possessing innate intelligence, seems obvious enough—if only because these instruments could not be used by anyone lacking it. The second, having "Law-based justice and moral virtue," reemphasizes the perspective of the Law adopted from the outset. Fundamental to the inquiry the Law deems obligatory is the idea that such inquiry is intended to gain cognizance of God. Sufficient intelligence to gain cognizance of anything must be accompanied by dedication to the principal task and directed as much to self-improvement as to dealings with others. The demand for moral virtue, consonant with what is prescribed by the Law, assures such dedication.

C. Demonstration accords with the Law
(§§11–36 [6.14–18.14])

As noted above, the third subpart consists of three smaller segments. In them, Averroës attempts first to prove that the Law calls to human beings by three methods (§11 [6.14–7.6]), then to establish that demonstration does not differ from what is set down in the Law (§§12–15 [7.17–9.17]), and finally to show that the philosophers are not guilty of unbelief (§§16–36 [9.18–18.14]). By far the largest of the subparts—to the point of being half as long as the entire treatise—the force of this one permits Averroës to summarize it in the next with language suggesting that the major goal of the treatise has now been accomplished.

1. Restating what has preceded as firmly settled ("determined") and positing the belief of the Muslim community in the truth of its divine Law, Averroës infers that the Law speaks to each Muslim in a manner suited to his or her temperament and nature. That belief, too, is qualified as "determined." What is more, cognizance of God and His creation is for the first time claimed to be happiness. No proof is offered for either statement. None is needed for the first, because the belief itself can be held by all only if each has some means of acceding to it. Precisely because the Law calls to all and people differ in nature, it must be able to reach all.[15] The second statement is part of a quiet, almost implicit, attempt to undermine one of al-Ghazālī's charges against the philosophers by showing that, far from denying the verses about the afterlife, they actually support and defend them.

2. In addition to exonerating the philosophers from charges of unbelief, Averroës endeavors to present their tools of reasoning as blameless (§12 [7.7–9]). The reasoning he employs to this end lacks lucidity and force, in part because it calls for too many steps. Four premises are posited—

(1) the Law is true, (2) the Law calls to demonstration ("reflection lead-ing to cognizance of the truth" being replaced with "demonstration"), (3) demonstration is true, and (4) truth does not contradict truth—from which it is deduced that demonstration does not contradict the Law. The syllogism is, nonetheless, a necessary preliminary to the idea of interpre-tation and thus to the reconciliation, sought shortly hereafter, between what is intellected and what is transmitted (see §14 [7.21–8.4]).

At issue are potential conflicts between reasoning—demonstrative or dialectical, although Averroës insists only upon the former—and the apparent sense of the Law, especially because figurative expressions are so prevalent in the latter. Averroës' solution, as contrasted with that of the theologians and their followers, promises to resolve the conflict while pre-serving the force of both the Law and reasoning. The tactic allows him to maintain his original goal of working within "the perspective of Law-based reflection" while questioning whether those who pose as defenders of the faith do not cause it harm. Specifically, he moves from affirming the oneness of truth—whether intellected or revealed and then handed down—to showing how interpretation safeguards the Law, and from that to the issue of consensus. First introduced to buttress the call for inter-pretation, the consideration of consensus subsequently permits Averroës to urge that the intentions of the philosophers are praiseworthy.

Acknowledgment of consensus among Muslims about the need to interpret some Qurʾānic verses opens the way for questioning which verses are to be interpreted and which are not (§15 [8.15–9.17]). To answer that question, Averroës restricts the domain of consensus by pointing to the eventual need within the community of Muslims to form something like a consensus about consensus, as well as by distinguishing practical from theoretical matters and explaining that the latter can never be a subject for consensus. In addition, he shifts the major theme from the interpretation of Qurʾānic verses to the discussion of the different positions pursued in the theoretical investigations of the philosophers.

3. The explicit defense of the philosophers is carried out by four different series of arguments. Averroës first faces the attack directly and attempts to show its inadequacy. For this he relies on the preceding dis-cussion, the inconsistency of al-Ghazālī's charges, the acceptance within the community of interpreting some Qurʾānic verses without detracting from respect for their apparent sense, and the need for precise speech about these kinds of questions (§§16–22 [9.18–13.16]). These are deemed sufficient for rescuing al-Fārābī and Avicenna from the accusations that their teachings about God's knowledge of particulars and the eternity of

the world constitute unbelief. Here, though, Averroës maintains silence about the charge concerning what they say with respect to the hereafter.

He begins this series of arguments by questioning the solidity of al-Ghazālī's charges (§16 [9.18–10.16]), then seeks to clarify what precisely the philosophers mean when they speak of divine knowledge (§17 [10.17–11.14]). The final part of the defense leads Averroës to concentrate mainly on the need for greater clarity about the use of language and to urge that some Qurʾānic verses must be interpreted if they are to be fully understood (§§18–22 [11.15–13.16]). Such a defense requires a more careful examination of interpretation, and it constitutes the next series of arguments in this segment (§§23–31 [13.17–16.19]). The examination itself consists of three, or possibly four, steps. First is the issue of the qualification needed for interpreting abstruse or recondite matters, there being no question that such matters are to be interpreted (§§23–24 [13.17–14.12]). Those qualified to interpret recondite matters have an obligation or responsibility to do so.

Not everything in the Law, however, is recondite; so the next step is to draw new limits concerning interpretation. For such verses, qualification to interpret means nothing (§§25–27 [14.13–15.16]). Unless everyone assents to some matters, there can be no community. The corollary is that ways to know and to accept or assent are present for all, except those who refuse through obstinacy or negligence. Yet nothing proves the truth of such matters—not even calling them roots. Clearly, though, one can deny them only by rejecting the primacy of the divine Law—that is, by rejecting the basic framework of the treatise.

At least some of what is to be accepted in this manner remains obscure; at most, such things can be talked about by means of examples or comparisons. But since it is assumed that such things are true with respect to the Law and that demonstration does not contradict the Law, there must also be a way to know whether they are true or not via demonstration. Because those skilled in demonstration have an obligation to interpret these matters, the argument returns to permissible interpretation and even to what must be interpreted by the qualified (§§28–30 [15.17–16.15]; also §31 [16.16–19]). A major part of this explanation thus focuses on delimiting the kinds of verses to be interpreted and identifying those suited to do so.

The starting point was: some verses are so difficult, abstruse, or recondite that they must be interpreted, but only by those qualified to do so. Then he noted that some verses, despite their difficulties, are to be taken in their apparent sense by all; others are to be taken in their apparent sense by some people and interpreted by others.[16] Averroës now seems ill at ease with this rule and seeks to refine it. Beginning again, he sets out the first two of three sorts *(aṣnāf)* of verses: the apparent admitting no interpretation, and the apparent to be interpreted by those adept at demonstration (§29 [15.21–16.4]). The reverse order permits him to illustrate the second sort more fully *(wa min hādhā al-ṣanf)* in the next section. Then, in the one following, he introduces a third sort: verses about which there is disagreement as to whether they can be interpreted or not.

The difference between the two enumerations is muted, even obfuscated, despite its importance. It turns on Averroës' unwillingness to acknowledge here that not all who concern themselves with the Law are adept at demonstration or even admit its value, much less that of interpretation. His quarrel here is more with those who admit interpretation but pay insufficient heed to how it must be limited, that is, who ignore "that the stop is at His saying (may He be exalted), 'None knows their interpretation but God'" (§30 [16.14]). Equally important, the tactic allows Averroës to return to the question passed over in silence here and in the previous segment—namely, what al-Fārābī and Avicenna say about the hereafter.

This topic is addressed in the next, or third, series of arguments (§§32–34 [16.20–17.14]) and has been prepared by the immediately preceding discussion—especially that of the last section. There is disagreement, claims Averroës, as to whether verses concerning the hereafter are to be taken literally or figuratively. In his eyes, however, nothing justifies dismissing them or categorizing them as politically expedient devices.[17]

As though replying to an objection about what has been set forth thus far, Averroës explains the difficulty of achieving a clear classification. The issue has become problematic because the authorities disagree among themselves, and al-Ghazālī appears unable to make up his own mind about the issue. An oblique reference to the preceding argument reminds the reader that rules for how learned people are to handle these verses have already been given (see §33 [17.6–7] with §23 [13.17–14.1] and §25 [14.13–14]). Another reference, equally oblique, points to what has been said about the need for those not learned to take such verses according to their apparent sense (§33 [17.9–10] and §34 [17.11–14] with §26 [14.18–15.8], §29 [16.4], and §30 [16.5–15]). The major emphasis throughout is on limiting such interpretations to those adept in demonstration and thus to preparing the final step in this series of arguments: blaming al-Ghazālī for having failed to do so.

In deed alone has he erred, however. After explaining that al-Ghazālī's penchant for discussing recondite matters in books directed to readers lacking the knowledge to interpret them has caused the community greater harm than that imputed to the philosophers, Averroës insists upon his famous predecessor being innocent of malice. Confused, to be sure, even overly eager to please all parties, al-Ghazālī was not ever intent upon harming his fellow Muslims. Nothing in his demeanor suggests he wished to do anything but help them (§35 [17.15–18.14]). At the very least, the exculpation is ambivalent. On the one hand, it makes al-Ghazālī appear impractical, if not simply foolish; on the other, it portrays him as far too desirous of approval or acclaim from others.[18]

The emphasis here on the way al-Ghazālī's actions vitiate his intentions prepares for a theme of central importance in the rest of the treatise. Though Averroës has spoken little thus far of intention, and only twice of intention with respect to the Law, that will become a major concern in the two major subparts of part two.[19] Although he meant to be helpful, al-Ghazālī caused harm—to the Law as well as to fellow Muslims, simple believers and learned philosophers alike. He erred because he did not pay attention to the differences among human beings or to the need to adjust his discourse accordingly. That is, he erred because he did not think about the intention of the Law and the methods set forth in it for addressing different kinds of people. His personal good intentions notwithstanding, al-Ghazālī contravened the intention of the Law.

The harm cannot be undone, but its effects can be limited. There is no need to ban all inquiry, nor will anything be gained by forbidding qualified individuals to study books in which philosophy, logic, and natural science are pursued. What is called for is greater attention to the intention of the Law and the methods by which it calls to human beings. An external restriction on al-Ghazālī's books, similar in kind to the internal one Averroës calls for in this whole subpart, would permit those capable of understanding al-Ghazālī's inquiries to read them yet bar from them others who are not so qualified. Those responsible for the well-being of the faithful—"the imams of the Muslims"—must couch their prohibitions in terms that respect the idea of the Law calling to all, albeit in different ways (§36 [18.5–14]).

D. Summary
(§37 [18.14–19])

According to Averroës, the presentation to this point has "established" two things: "the discussion between the Law and wisdom" and also "the statutes for interpreting the Law." What he means by the latter is clear, and he terms the former a "type of reflection." The reflection or discussion thus far has been methodological or procedural rather than substantive. Arguing always "from the perspective of Law-based reflection" (§1 [1.7]), Averroës has affirmed a consonance between what philosophy does and aims at and what the Law urges be done. To this end, he has cited passages of the Law and spoken generally about the subjects philosophy inquires into as well as the means by which it does so. By means of analogies drawn between practices accepted in the juridical pursuit of the Law and what is needed with respect to the study of philosophy and its logical methods, he has pleaded for permitting the latter. Finally, in turning to "the statutes for interpreting the Law," he has insisted upon the absence of contradiction between whatever is reached when the best method of philosophical investigation is pursued and what is set forth in the Law.

Yet, believers in the Law can and do point to differences between it and the results reached by philosophical inquiry. Averroës, however, has argued tenaciously that such criticisms are based on misunderstanding what the philosophers have said. Differently stated, he has shown that there is no "discussion *between* the Law and wisdom" (my emphasis); when they speak, they say the same thing. Why, then, does Averroës continue the *Decisive Treatise?*

He does so because the inferences from the Law drawn to this point are not fully persuasive. Plausible arguments have been made, but nothing has been determined or established—Averroës' assertions to the contrary notwithstanding. In what follows, he will speak of the intention of the Law and the Lawgiver. By showing that their intention can be achieved only when the methods set forth in the Law for addressing the various kinds of human beings are followed, and that this understanding of discourse or discussion is precisely that set forth among the philosophers, he completes the argument of the first part.

E. The intent of the Law and its methods
(§§38–51 [18.19–23.18])

This subpart is divided into three smaller parts or segments. In the first, Averroës expounds upon the intention of the Law ([§§38–39 [18.19–19.17]]), while in the second he explains how that intention is achieved (§§40–43 [19.18–21.3]). This leads him to explore in the third how the Law seeks to address all people, regardless of their natural capacities (§§44–51 [21.4–23.18]). Thus, the latter two segments bring

Averroës back to themes of earlier discussions—in particular, that focused on the inclusiveness of the divine Law and the one undermining al-Ghazālī's procedure, along with that of other theologians.

1. At the beginning of this subpart, Averroës alerts his addressee to the importance he attaches to the subject at hand by declaring, for the first and only time in the *Decisive Treatise*, that here is something "you ought to know"[20]—namely, that "what is intended by the Law is only to teach true science and true practice." Defining true science as "cognizance of God," of "all the existing things as they are," and of "happiness . . . and of misery in the hereafter," he presents the Law as providing the all-important cognizance of the hereafter that philosophy has not been shown to provide. Moreover, insofar as the Law makes us acquainted with true practice, it brings about (or at least intends to bring about) unity between knowledge and action.

While explaining the domain of true practice, Averroës pauses momentarily to speak of al-Ghazālī and what he sought to do in his famous book, *Iḥyāʾ ʿulūm al-dīn* (The revival of the sciences of religion). However, calling this a digression, Averroës returns to the theme of the Law teaching true science and practice. The digression concerns "actions of the soul"—that is, "moral habits that the Law calls to or bans"— rather than "bodily actions." Concerned that people had become too engrossed in the latter, al-Ghazālī had intended his book to redirect their attention to the former. Of the two, notes Averroës, this is the type "more involved with piety, which is the cause of happiness."

Only toward the end of this subpart[21] is the reader able to discern the significance of the digression. There, too, Averroës makes what at first appears to be an awkward argument. It has to do with his identification of piety as health of the soul and as what the Lawgiver intends by his Law. Consonant with his provoking parallel between the physician and the Lawgiver, and even with the opening sentence of the next section ("from this it has become evident to you that sound interpretations— not to mention corrupt ones—must not be established in books for the multitude"), the whole presentation nonetheless remains vague and unfocused. When both references to piety are put together, however, the discerning reader understands just how al-Ghazālī's penchant for discussing the wrong subjects in popular writings caused more harm than benefit to his fellow Muslims.

2. Addressed to all and intended to teach true science and practice to all, the Law contains different methods for achieving these ends. Too often, the primary intention of the Law—namely, "taking care of the

greater number without neglecting to alert the select [few]" (§40 [19.20–21])—is neglected. Given such disparity among the natural capacities of people and thus the impossibility of all having the same degree of understanding or being open to the same methods of instruction, the Law must have different ways to speak to these dissimilar interlocutors. That is, the Law must admit of interpretation.

Averroës' somewhat technical account of the various instructional methods used in the Law is aimed at showing how it communicates a single message to these differing capacities (§41 [20.2–14]). Presented as four different kinds of syllogisms, these methods are brought back to the three instances of the first enumeration noted above: arguments admitting of no interpretation whatever, arguments admitting of interpretation generally, and arguments admitting of interpretation only by those qualified. Now, for the first time, Averroës admits the possibility of popular interpretations—but this with the caveat that they be made for the multitude, not by them, and with a clear indication of how tentative is the admission (§43 [20.19–21.3]).[22]

3. Why Averroës places such emphasis on the intention of the Law and the way it speaks to all the people comes to light once he begins to point out how those who fail to discern this intention and use the wrong kind of speech in speaking to the multitude actually lead them astray— that is, to unbelief—and that leading others to unbelief is itself a form of unbelief. Singling out al-Ghazālī by name, Averroës explains that those who take no notice of the different methods in the Law or ignore that "people are of three sorts with respect to the Law" are to be deemed guilty of such a wrong. Indeed, they are the ones who declare demonstrative or otherwise recondite interpretations to the many not able to receive them. The charge emphatically does not apply to the philosophers, for Averroës has shown them to be ever circumspect about what they say to the many. Unbelief comes about because the one to whom a difficult interpretation is declared must reject the apparent sense of what is interpreted and then go on to establish the interpretation. By definition, such individuals are unable to grasp the eventual interpretation. Thus, they find themselves in the position of having rejected the apparent sense without having gained anything with which to replace it (§45 [21.10–15]).

The point is that some matters in the Law are of such difficulty they should be presented to the rhetorical sort of people as though they do not admit of interpretation; the same holds for other matters that cannot be explained by rhetorical means (§46 [21.16–21] with §§39–40 [19.10–20.1]). To emphasize this point, Averroës returns to the famous question of where the stop is to be placed with respect to Qur'ān 3:7 and urges, as he did earlier (§30 [16.12–15]), that it be after "none knows their interpretation but God."[23] Here, as there, Averroës is intent upon showing that some verses should not be interpreted by the many, that to do so merely leads them to unbelief. To strengthen his case, he evokes the image of the Lawgiver once again and claims that to present the many with interpretation is, in effect, to call them to unbelief and thus to contravene the Lawgiver's call to the Law (§47 [21.21–22.7]). In sum, this discourse on the Lawgiver's call and that in the next section on the Lawgiver's intention in that call, like his earlier account of the Law's intention (§38 [18.19–19.1]), allow Averroës to set the record straight on unbelief. Now, however, he moves beyond attempts to exculpate the philosophers by inculpating their accusers—in particular, al-Ghazālī and the theologians.[24]

Lest his goal here be misunderstood, Averroës resorts to a rhetorical image or parable of his own: He who declares interpretations to those not apt to receive them is like one who dissuades people from following a physician, whereas the physician urges them to adopt actions for preserving health and avoiding sickness, this other person causes them to become sick (§48 [22.8–18]). Like the physician, the Lawgiver seeks the health of the people—the health of their souls. Hence, to claim that what he says is not true on the surface and can be interpreted amounts to dissuading the people from pursuing the health of their souls. Because those who make this claim neglect to add that only certain people under certain conditions may seek to interpret the Law, they lead the many into sickness. Part of their error is their failure to consider the intention of the Lawgiver. Putting their own intention first and failing to ask about that of the Lawgiver, they lead astray even when their interpretation and intention are sound. When these are unsound, they risk leading the people to doubt whether there is health or sickness, or even whether there are things conducive to health and such as to avert sickness (§49 [22.19–23.3]).

Averroës insists that his image or parable is very accurate, even certain (§50 [23.4–14]). What gives it this status is the link between the physician and the Lawgiver; for the health of souls to which the Lawgiver aspires is piety—namely, the piety that was linked with true practice, the teaching of which was said to be intended by the Law, and whose mention prompted Averroës to admit that he had digressed from his exposition (§38 [19.4–6, 9]). How philosophy provides the best understanding of the intention of the Law and the Lawgiver and ensures that it will be followed by the people has now been shown. In addition, the critics of philosophy have been revealed to be incapable both of discerning that intention and of furthering it. Averroës now brings the argument full circle by affirming that knowledge of the health intended by the Lawgiver is precisely what is needed for happiness in the hereafter. As is now perfectly evident, only the philosopher proves himself able to speak to such happiness and to urge the many to seek it in accordance with the intention of the Lawgiver and the Law. And, according to Averroës, only the philosopher is capable of sound interpretation—that is, of "the deposit mankind was charged with holding and held" (§51 [23.15–18]).

F. On factions within Islam
(§§52–58 [23.19–25.19])

Confident that his account of philosophy—its aspirations and accomplishments—adequately shows it to be an important ally of the Law and that none of the charges against those known to have engaged in it is warranted, Averroës can now turn to a consideration of how it has come to be so little esteemed. He begins the consideration with an explanation of what has prompted contending groups or factions to arise within the Islamic community and why they trouble the life of otherwise tranquil Muslims (§§52–54 [23.19–24.13]). Then, in keeping with the general attempt throughout the treatise to provide a remedy for such ills, Averroës turns to an examination of what can be done to avoid the ones to which these groups give rise (§§55–58 [24.14–25.19]). Nothing here is based on the introduction of new evidence; to the contrary, like any competent legal counselor, Averroës does no more than draw the consequences from the principles presented thus far.

1. Contending groups or factions emerged for two reasons. First at issue between one group and another was the difference over the way verses in the Law were to be interpreted. Then they began to disagree over whether the interpretations were to be promulgated and, if so, to whom. That the factions arose at all is bad enough; what compounded the problem was that the different groups carried their quarreling to the people and thus threw the community into turmoil. Even then, their ignorance of the way people of differing capacities are to be addressed led to disruption and strife. It is an ignorance that concerns the methods and, more important, the intention of the Law: such people—and here Averroës names only two schools of theologians—are woefully misinformed about the way to present arguments to the many and even about the conditions for sound argument. They rely upon patently false methods of reasoning, he claims, and seem not to be aware of their error.

The dissension caused by the ignorance of these troublemakers is compounded by their belligerence. Ever ready to label those who deviate from their methods as unbelievers, they prove only how little they understand that the Lawgiver's mission is to address and attract rather than to rebuke and drive away. Through him and his endorsement of methods suited to the varying capacities of the different kinds of believers, the Law calls to all. Nothing in the Law or in the conduct of the Lawgiver buttresses their insisting solely on their way or their method.

2. Simply stated, those responsible for the breaking out of factions fail to understand that there is no need to improve upon the Law. It indicates clearly and repeatedly that there are three methods to be followed for persuading the people: two for the majority and one for the select few. The methods to be used with the majority are the shared ones—that is, rhetoric and dialectic. Demonstration is to be used only with the select. Consequently, there is no room for the sophistical methods adopted by the Ash°arites (see §55 [24.14–20] with §53 [24.5]).

Restricting the argument more here—even putting his own position at peril—Averroës goes on to claim that there is really very little need for interpretation. Not practiced in the early days of Islam, its advent was accompanied by a decrease in piety and an increase in intercommunal strife. Still, this cannot be his last word. He has placed far too much emphasis heretofore on the need for interpretation, both to understand the Law and to discern why the philosophers are not guilty of the charges brought against them by al-Ghazālī.

The overstatement serves to preserve respect for the apparent sense of the Law. Averroës is proposing an antidote to the rush to interpretation—especially to sophistical interpretation—that first brought about the strife deplored so here. In restricting interpretation now to those skilled at demonstration, he merely emphasizes more stringently what he has said heretofore. The urgency of the crisis that prompted him to write this treatise finds expression in his admonition about what "we are responsible for believing."[25] That is, the perspective guiding Averroës' reflection in this work from the outset requires him to restrict his speech and even his inquiry. Insofar as he or any other philosopher speaks as a member of the Muslim community, it is necessary to acquiesce in, or assent to, certain beliefs. To restrict interpretation in this fashion is part of that obligation or responsibility.

Having shown thus far in this subpart how much the theologians are to be blamed for the factions that trouble the community, Averroës brings it and the larger argument of the *Decisive Treatise* to a close by showing how a more thoughtful theology might better defend the Qur°ān and thereby the Law. It need only pay more attention to the unique character of the way the Qur°ān speaks to all. The theologians have sought to improve upon the Qur°ān with their own examples, but in doing so they have by no means come close to the richness of the methods and examples to be found in the Qur°ān itself. They seem unaware that chief among the features placing it beyond imitability is that the statements found in it are "completely persuasive and able to bring about assent for everyone," "admit of defense, ending up at a point where no one grasps an interpretation of them ... except those adept in demonstration," and alert "those adept in the truth to the true interpretation" (§58 [25.14–17]).

G. Conclusion
(§§59–60 [25.20–26.14])

Though Averroës is now ready to bring this exposition to a close, he recognizes that he has by no means exhausted the subject. It is his desire to write more about "this intention"—that is, in this context, the intention of the Law. More needs to be said about how it teaches true science and true practice—that is, "true interpretation"—and also about the way it provides persuasion for all the people. Now, however, he acknowledges for the first time that part of the harm befalling the Law has come from those associated with its milk sister, philosophy. The acknowledgment is belated and cursory—as well it must be, lest he be forced to begin again the earlier defense of philosophy and the philosophers. Nor is anything more than this passing acknowledgment requisite, for Averroës has clearly indicated throughout the *Decisive Treatise* how philosophy must and can work together with the Law. The considerations informing such cooperation are ultimately linked to an understanding of the way human beings are to live, to their governance, as Averroës intimates with his final words of gratitude to his ruler and of admonition to both the theologians and the philosophers.

IV. Conclusion

The preceding explanatory interpretation of the *Decisive Treatise* urges that philosophy or wisdom—at least as expressed by Averroës and those with whom he associates himself within the medieval Islamic tradition— has the same intention with respect to governance as the Law, that both seek to provide for the well-being of all to the extent possible. So stated, the agreement between the two depends in no way upon determining to what extent individual philosophers privately assent to the Law, nor in probing the sincerity of their various efforts to buttress its claims. The reasoning leading to this interpretation looks, rather, to what is required for sound political life—and this in terms both of lasting conditions and of those that arise with the ascendancy of rule proclaiming itself to be guided by revelation. In this respect, it self-consciously introduces a new stage in the perennial reflection on the relationship between religion and philosophy, or between the divine Law and wisdom.[26] No privileged presuppositions support this approach. It is grounded simply in a desire to explain the writing as it has come down to us, and to do so by relying solely on arguments presented by Averroës himself.

To recognize similarity, perhaps identity, of intention between the Law and wisdom leaves open the larger question of what each intends. For now, it must remain so. Though Averroës has identified in outline what the Law intends and has shown the ways in which wisdom agrees with that intention, he has done nothing to plumb the content of that intention. Nor was that, finally, part of the task he took upon himself here. A complete investigation of true science and true practice belongs, as he has clearly noted, to other discussions and to other kinds of writings. Averroës has made the reasons for confining such kinds of inquiry to these other writings amply clear, while noting here that science, or knowledge, and practice are inseparable.

Translator's Introduction
to the *Epistle Dedicatory*

I. The *Epistle*'s title and its place

In Marcus Joseph Müller's *Philosophie und Theologie von Averroes*, the *Decisive Treatise* is presented as the first part of a trilogy, the other two parts being the *Kashf ʿan manāhij al-adilla fī ʿaqāʾid al-milla* (Uncovering the methods of proofs with respect to the beliefs of the religious community) and the epistle presented here. Although it was placed in the Arabic manuscript between the *Decisive Treatise* and the *Uncovering*, Müller moved the epistle to the end of both works and titled it *Ḍamīma*, or Appendix, while keeping as a subtitle the title assigned by the scribe of the manuscript: *The Question the Shaykh Abū al-Walīd Mentioned in the Decisive Treatise*. And so it remained, albeit with momentary hesitation by at least one translator, until Muhsin Mahdi showed convincingly why this little writing should properly be considered an "Epistle Dedicatory" to the other two treatises. Mahdi's argument is so straightforward and persuasive that one can only wonder why no earlier scholar had noticed the anomaly of calling this epistle an appendix and treating it as such.

Averroës mentions this writing and its general subject matter in the text of the *Decisive Treatise* as something he has already completed—that is, as a question to which he has already responded. He does precisely the same with respect to the *Decisive Treatise* and its subject matter in the *Uncovering*. What is more, Müller and other scholars understood the references to the *Decisive Treatise* in the *Uncovering* to indicate that it must therefore be a sequel to that writing. Precisely the same reasoning leads to the conclusion that this little work is an epistle intended as a preface to the *Decisive Treatise*, not as an appendix to it and the *Uncovering*.[1]

It has no title, for the simple reason that epistles dedicatory are usually not accorded any. We know the work, instead, for what it is—for its subject matter. It is a letter, addressed to a particular person, in which the question of God's knowledge of particulars is examined, this in order to prepare the discussion of the relationship between the divine Law and wisdom or philosophy carried out in the *Decisive Treatise,* as well as the larger inquiry Averroës adumbrates at its end. There, he expresses his hope to investigate at greater length the intention of the divine Law, especially how it teaches true science and true practice—that is, true interpretation—and how it provides persuasion for all the people. Indeed, in addition to the precision of the title—*Kashf ʿan manāhij al-adilla fī ʿaqāʾid al-milla* (Uncovering the methods of proofs with respect to the beliefs of the religious community)—Averroës adds a subtitle to make his goals in this work even more explicit: *Wa taʿrīf mā waqaʿa fīhā bi-ḥasab al-taʾwīl min al-shubah al-muzayyifa wa al-bidaʿ al-muḍalla* (Making cognizable the obscurities that foster deviation and the innovations that lead astray occurring in them [the beliefs] from interpretation). Clearly, this last work is as much a popular work as the *Decisive Treatise.* What, then, of the *Epistle Dedicatory?*

II. The argument of the *Epistle Dedicatory*

This missive is dedicated to a particular individual, one whom Averroës never names and to whom he always refers by the polite and formal second-person plural form of address. That is not the form Averroës uses when responding to putative objections in the *Decisive Treatise,* nor when explaining what ought to be clear to his particular interlocutor there. No; there, as well as in the *Uncovering,* the form of address used is the more familiar second-person singular. The addressee of this small writing is, moreover, someone for whom Averroës may appropriately beseech God to prolong his might or power, someone who is gifted with "excellent discernment" as well as a "noble nature" (§§1–2 [128.4–5]). It is also someone with whom Averroës has already conversed about the question investigated here (§5 [129.15]), someone with a sufficient grasp of the question and of the position of the philosophers with respect to it that Averroës can dispense with preliminaries and move directly to the core of the question. The addressee is also a person interested in the resolution of the doubt, an individual who wants to understand how the conflict between the dialectical theologians and the philosophers with respect to God's knowledge of particulars can be resolved. The one person who comes to mind once all of these attributes are listed is none other than the Almohade sovereign to whom Averroës seems to refer at the end of the *Decisive Treatise*—namely, Abū Yaʿqūb Yūsuf.

But why, given all we know about the close relationship Averroës enjoyed with his sovereign, would he raise this question as one with which to open this trilogy? The answer, as becomes evident in the *Decisive Treatise,* is that the charges brought by al-Ghazālī against the philosophers have attracted so much attention that a public response is now appropriate. Averroës opens the trilogy with a defense of the philosophers and their approach to the question of God's knowledge of particulars—a defense grounded in a demonstration that the approach followed by the dialectical theologians leads to confusion—in order to indicate that the work to follow seeks to protect the divine Law and its teaching, not to undermine it.

The epistle seems to consist of five major parts. After an introduction that takes account of the doubt this question of eternal knowledge has engendered in the addressee, Averroës explains that he will first provide a clear explanation of the problem, then provide a solution to it (§2 [128.5–8]). The problem—the same one that is alluded to in the *Decisive Treatise* (§17 [10.17–11.14])—concerns God's knowledge, to be sure, but also the difference between human knowledge and divine knowledge as well as the question of whether things change when they come into existence after having not existed. If they do change, how can eternal knowledge be one and the same? If they do not, how can we speak of a difference between what is and what is not (§3 [128.9–17])? In the next two sections (§4–5 [129.4–15]), Averroës passes in review additional considerations with respect to the question, then turns to the promised solution. It, too, is set forth in two sections (§6–7 [129.16–130.17]).

Though a proper solution to the question would require a long discussion, Averroës acknowledges that this is not the place for it. He focuses, instead, on the rhetorical weakness in the solution that al-Ghazālī set forth in his *Incoherence of the Philosophers* and then points to the proper solution, one that distinguishes between eternal knowledge—which is proper to God—and the generated knowledge that is proper to human beings. It depends upon knowing how to draw a correct analogy between these two kinds of knowledge; it depends, that is, upon knowing how to reason correctly about them. The philosophers, who do understand logic and its limits, are able to draw the correct analogy.

Having solved the problem, Averroës turns to a consideration of what this means for our understanding of the way God knows things, as contrasted to the way we know things (§8–9 [130.18–131.6]), and then concludes by affirming that the philosophers would never have explained matters as al-Ghazālī and the dialectical theologians claim (§10 [131.7–13]). They would not have done so—indeed, they could not have done so—because that would oblige them to deny that eternal knowledge includes particulars. Yet anyone even remotely aware of the teaching of the philosophers knows that they attribute the insight gained by means of dreams and other kinds of inspiration to precisely such knowledge of particulars.

The introduction and the conclusion are roughly equal in length, as are the statement of the problem and its solution plus the statement of what that solution entails. Differently stated, there is to be found in this short *Epistle Dedicatory* a symmetry in the formal structure of the argument that meshes with the symmetry found in its simple, almost rhetorical, character. An alert reader sees readily that the doubt has not been sufficiently laid to rest, but discerns as well that the path of the philosophers as presented here by Averroës is more salutary for those who would live by the precepts of divine Law than the path of the dialectical theologians, at least as it appears from al-Ghazālī's attempts to criticize the philosophers. A sovereign intent upon ruling intelligently a community that looks to revealed law for guidance would do well to pay close attention to the teachings of the philosophers rather than to those of the dialectical theologians. And, as we know, the treatise that follows immediately thereafter will show yet other reasons for heeding such a lesson.

THE BOOK OF THE

DECISIVE TREATISE,

DETERMINING THE CONNECTION

BETWEEN THE LAW AND WISDOM

◆

In the name of God, the Merciful and the Compassionate.
May God be prayed to for Muḥammad and his family,
and may they be accorded peace.

[i. Introduction]

(1) The jurist, imam, judge, and uniquely learned Abū al-Walīd
Muḥammad ibn Aḥmad ibn Rushd (may God be pleased with him) said:
Praise be to God with all praises, and a prayer for Muḥammad, His chosen
servant and messenger. Now, the goal of this statement is for us to investigate, from the perspective of Law-based[1] reflection, whether reflection
upon philosophy and the sciences of logic is permitted, prohibited, or
commanded—and this as a recommendation or as an obligation—by
the Law.

[ii. That philosophy and logic are obligatory]

[A. That philosophy is obligatory]

(2) So we say: If the activity of philosophy is nothing more than
reflection upon existing things and consideration of them insofar as they
are an indication of the Artisan—I mean insofar as they are artifacts,
for existing things indicate the Artisan only through cognizance[2] of the
art in them, and the more complete cognizance of the art in them
is, the more complete is cognizance of the Artisan—and if the Law has

كتاب فصل المقال

وتقرير ما بين الشريعة والحكمة من الاتصال

بسم الله الرحمان الرحيم

وصلى الله على محمد وعلى آله وسلم.

(١) قال الفقيه الإمام القاضي العلامة الأوحد أبو الوليد محمد بن أحمد بن رشد رضي الله عنه: أما بعد حمد الله بجميع محامده والصلاة على محمد عبده المصطفى ورسوله، فإن الغرض في هذا القول أن نفحص على جهة النظر الشرعي هل النظر في الفلسفة وعلوم المنطق مباح بالشرع أم محظور أم مأمور به، إما على جهة الندب أو على جهة الوجوب.

(٢) فنقول: إن كان فعل الفلسفة ليس شيئا أكثر من النظر في الموجودات واعتبارها من جهة دلالتها على الصانع – أعني من جهة ما هي مصنوعات، فإن الموجودات إنما تدل على الصانع بمعرفة صنعتها وإنه كلما كانت المعرفة بصنعتها أتم كانت المعرفة

١

recommended and urged consideration of existing things, then it is evident that what this name indicates is either obligatory or recommended
by the Law.

    That the Law calls for consideration of existing things by means of
5   the intellect and for pursuing cognizance of them by means of it is evi-
dent from various | verses in the Book of God (may He be blessed and
exalted).[3] There is His statement (may He be exalted), "Consider, you
who have sight" [59:2]; this is a text for the obligation of using both
intellectual and Law-based syllogistic reasoning.[4] And there is His state-
10   ment (may He be exalted), "Have they not reflected upon the kingdoms
of the heavens and the earth and what things God has created?" [7:185];
this is a text urging reflection upon all existing things. And God (may
He be exalted) has made it known that one of those whom He selected
and venerated by means of this knowledge was Abraham (peace upon
15   him); thus, He (may He be exalted) said, "And in this way we made
Abraham see the kingdoms of the heavens and the earth, that he might
be . . ." [and so on to the end of] the verse [6:75].[5] And He (may He be
exalted) said, "Do they not reflect upon the camels, how they have been
created, and upon the heaven, how it has been raised up?" [88:17]. And
20   He said, "And they ponder the creation of the heavens and the earth"
[3:191]—and so on, in innumerable other verses.

[B. The case for syllogistic reasoning]

    (3) Since it has been determined that the Law makes it obligatory to
reflect upon existing things by means of the intellect, and to consider them;
and consideration is nothing more than inferring and drawing out the
25   unknown from the known; and this is syllogistic reasoning or by means of
syllogistic reasoning, therefore, it is obligatory that we go about reflecting
upon the existing things by means of intellectual syllogistic reasoning.
And it is evident that this manner of reflection the Law calls for and

بالصانع أتم – وكان الشرع قد ندب إلى اعتبار الموجودات وحث على ذلك، فبيّن أن ما يدل عليه هذا الاسم إما واجب بالشرع وإما مندوب.

فأما أن الشرع دعا إلى اعتبار الموجودات بالعقل وتطلّب معرفتها به، فذلك بيّن في غير [٢] ما آية من كتاب الله تبارك وتعالى. مثل قوله تعالى ﴿فَٱعْتَبِرُواْ يَٰٓأُوْلِى ٱلْأَبْصَٰرِ﴾ [٢:٥٩]، وهذا نص على وجوب استعمال القياس العقلي والشرعي معا. ومثل قوله تعالى ﴿أَوَلَمْ يَنظُرُواْ فِى مَلَكُوتِ ٱلسَّمَٰوَٰتِ وَٱلْأَرْضِ وَمَا خَلَقَ ٱللَّهُ مِنْ شَىْءٍ﴾ [١٨٥:٧]، وهذا نص بالحث على النظر في جميع الموجودات. وأعلم الله تعالى أنَّ ممن خصه بهذا العلم وشرفه به إبراهيم عليه السلام، فقال تعالى ﴿وَكَذَٰلِكَ نُرِى إِبْرَٰهِيمَ مَلَكُوتَ ٱلسَّمَٰوَٰتِ وَٱلْأَرْضِ وَلِيَكُونَ...﴾ الآية [٧٥:٦]، وقال تعالى ﴿أَفَلَا يَنظُرُونَ إِلَى ٱلْإِبِلِ كَيْفَ خُلِقَتْ وَإِلَى ٱلسَّمَآءِ كَيْفَ رُفِعَتْ﴾ [١٧-١٨:٨٨]، وقال ﴿وَيَتَفَكَّرُونَ فِى خَلْقِ ٱلسَّمَٰوَٰتِ وَٱلْأَرْضِ﴾ [١٩١:٣]، إلى غير ذلك من الآيات التي لا تُحصى كثرة.

(٣) وإذا تقرر أن الشرع قد أوجب النظر بالعقل في الموجودات واعتبارها، وكان الاعتبار ليس شيئا أكثر من استنباط المجهول من المعلوم واستخراجه منه، وهذا هو القياس أو بالقياس، فواجب أن نجعل نظرنا في الموجودات بالقياس العقلي. وبيّن أن

urges is the most complete kind of reflection by means of the most complete kind of syllogistic reasoning and is the one called "demonstration."

(4) Since the Law has urged cognizance of God (may He be exalted) and of all of the things existing through Him by means of demonstration; and it is preferable—or even necessary—that anyone who wants to know God (may He be blessed and exalted) and all of the existing things by means of demonstration set out first to know the kinds of demonstrations, their conditions, and in what [way] demonstrative syllogistic reasoning differs from dialectical, rhetorical, and sophistical syllogistic reasoning; and that is not possible unless, prior to that, he sets out to become cognizant of what unqualified syllogistic reasoning is, how many kinds of it there are, and which of them is syllogistic reasoning and which not; and that is not possible either unless, prior to that, he sets out to become cognizant of the parts of which syllogistic reasoning is composed— I mean, the premises and their kinds—therefore, the one who has faith[6] in the Law and follows its command to reflect upon existing things perhaps comes under the obligation to set out, before reflecting, to become cognizant of these things whose status | with respect to reflection is that of tools to work.

For just as the jurist infers from the command to obtain juridical understanding of the statutes the obligation to become cognizant of the kinds of juridical syllogistic reasoning and which of them is syllogistic reasoning and which not, so, too, is it obligatory for the one cognizant [of God] to infer from the command to reflect upon the beings the obligation to become cognizant of intellectual syllogistic reasoning and its kinds. Nay, it is even more fitting that he do so; for if the jurist infers from His statement (may He be exalted), "Consider, you who have sight" [59:2], the obligation to become cognizant of juridical syllogistic reasoning, then how much more fitting is it that the one cognizant of God infer from that the obligation to become cognizant of intellectual syllogistic reasoning.

هذا النحو من النظر الذي دعا إليه الشرع وحث عليه هو أتم أنواع النظر بأتم أنواع القياس وهو المسمى ((برهانا)).

(٤) وإذا كان الشرع قد حث على معرفة الله تعالى وسائر موجوداته بالبرهان، وكان من الأفضل أو الأمر الضروري لمن أراد أن يعلم الله تبارك وتعالى وسائر الموجودات بالبرهان أن يتقدم أوّلًا فيعلم أنواع البراهين وشروطها وبماذا يخالف القياس البرهاني القياس الجدلي والقياس الخطابي والقياس المغالطي، وكان لا يمكن ذلك دون أن يتقدم فيعرف قبل ذلك ما هو القياس المطلق وكم أنواعه وما منه قياس وما منه ليس بقياس، وذلك لا يمكن أيضا إلا ويتقدم فيعرف قبل ذلك أجزاء القياس التي منها تركب – أعني المقدمات وأنواعها – فقد يجب على المؤمن بالشرع الممتثل أمره بالنظر في الموجودات أن يتقدم قبل النظر فيعرف هذه الأشياء التي تتنزل [٣] من النظر منزلة الآلات من العمل.

فإنه كما أن الفقيه يستنبط من الأمر بالتفقه في الأحكام وجوب معرفة المقاييس الفقهية على أنواعها وما منها قياس وما منها ليس بقياس، كذلك يجب على العارف أن يستنبط من الأمر بالنظر في الموجودات وجوب معرفة القياس العقلي وأنواعه، بل هو أحرى بذلك لأنه إذا كان الفقيه يستنبط من قوله تعالى ((فَٱعْتَبِرُوا۟ يَٰٓأُو۟لِى ٱلْأَبْصَٰرِ)) [٢:٥٩] وجوب معرفة القياس الفقهي فكم بالحري أن يستنبط من ذلك العارف بالله وجوب معرفة القياس العقلي.

It is not for someone to say, "Now, this kind of reflection about intellectual syllogistic reasoning is a heretical innovation, since it did not exist
in the earliest days [of Islam]." For reflection upon juridical syllogistic
reasoning and its kinds is also something inferred after the earliest days,
5   yet it is not opined to be a heretical innovation. So it is obligatory to
believe the same about reflection upon intellectual syllogistic reasoning—
and for this there is a reason, but this is not the place to mention it.
Moreover, most of the adherents to this religion support intellectual
syllogistic reasoning, except for a small group of strict literalists, and
10   they are refuted by the texts [of the Qurʾān].

(5) Since it has been determined that the Law makes reflection upon
intellectual syllogistic reasoning and its kinds obligatory, just as it makes
reflection upon juridical syllogistic reasoning obligatory, therefore, it is
evident that, if someone prior to us has not set out to investigate intel-
15   lectual syllogistic reasoning and its kinds, it is obligatory for us to begin
to investigate it and for the one who comes after to rely upon the one who
preceded,[7] so that cognizance of it might be perfected. For it is difficult
or impossible for one person to grasp all that he needs of this by himself
and from the beginning, just as it is difficult for one person to infer all
20   he needs to be cognizant of concerning the kinds of juridical syllogistic
reasoning. Nay, this is even more the case with being cognizant of intellectual syllogistic reasoning.

(6) If someone other than us has already investigated that, it is evi-
dently obligatory for us to rely on what the one who has preceded us says
25   about what we are pursuing, regardless of whether that other person
shares our religion or not. For when a valid sacrifice is performed by
means of a tool, | no consideration is given, with respect to the validity
of the sacrifice, as to whether the tool belongs to someone who shares in
our religion or not, so long as it fulfills the conditions for validity. And by
30   "not sharing [in our religion]," I mean those Ancients who reflected upon
these things before the religion of Islam.

وليس لِقَائِلٍ أن يقول إن هذا النوع من النظر في القياس العقلي بدعة إذ لم يكن في الصدر الأول. فإن النظر أيضا في القياس الفقهي وأنواعه هو شيء استُنبط بعد الصدر الأول وليس يُرى أنه بدعة، فكذلك يجب أن يُعتقَد في النظر في القياس العقلي – ولهذا سبب ليس هذا موضع ذكره – بل أكثر أصحاب هذه الملة مثبتون القياس العقلي إلا طائفة من الحشوية قليلة وهم محجوجون بالنصوص.

(٥) فإذا تقرر أنه يجب بالشرع النظر في القياس العقلي وأنواعه كما يجب النظر في القياس الفقهي، فبيّن أنه إن كان لم يتقدم أحد ممن قبلنا بفحص عن القياس العقلي وأنواعه أنه يجب علينا أن نبتدئ بالفحص عنه وأن يستعين في ذلك المتأخر بالمتقدم حتى تكمل المعرفة به. فإنه عسير أو غير ممكن أن يقف واحد من الناس من تلقائه وابتداءً على جميع ما يحتاج إليه من ذلك، كما أنه عسير أن يستنبط واحد جميع ما يحتاج إليه من معرفة أنواع القياس الفقهي، بل معرفة القياس العقلي أحرى بذلك.

(٦) وإن كان غيرنا قد فحص عن ذلك، فبيّن أنه يجب علينا أن نستعين على ما نحن بسبيله بما قاله من تقدمنا في ذلك وسواء كان ذلك الغير مشاركا لنا في الملة أو غير مشارك. فإن الآلة التي تصح بها التذكية [٤] ليس يُعتبَر في صحة التذكية بها كونها آلة لمشارك لنا في الملة أو غير مشارك إذا كانت فيها شروط الصحة – وأعني بغير المشارك من نظر في هذه الأشياء من القدماء قبل ملة الإسلام.

(7) Since this is the case—and all that is needed with respect to reflection about the matter of intellectual syllogistic reasonings has been investigated by the Ancients in the most complete manner—therefore, we ought perhaps to seize their books in our hands and reflect upon what they have said about that. And if it is all correct, we will accept it from them; whereas, if there is anything not correct in it, we will alert [people] to it.

(8) Since we have finished with this type of reflection and have acquired the tools by which we are able to consider existing things and the indication of artfulness in them—for one who is not cognizant of the artfulness is not cognizant of what has been artfully made, and one who is not cognizant of what has been artfully made is not cognizant of the Artisan—therefore, it is perhaps obligatory that we start investigating existing things according to the order and manner we have gained from the art of becoming cognizant about demonstrative syllogisms. It is evident, moreover, that this goal is completed for us with respect to existing things only when they are investigated successively by one person after another and when, in doing so, the one coming after makes use of the one having preceded—along the lines of what occurs in the mathematical sciences.

For if we were to assume the art of geometry and, likewise, the art of astronomy to be nonexistent in this time of ours, and if a single man wished to discern on his own the sizes of the heavenly bodies, their shapes, and their distances from one another, that would not be possible for him—for example, to become cognizant of the size of the sun with respect to the earth and of other things about the sizes of the planets— not even if he were by nature the most intelligent person, unless it were by means of revelation or something resembling revelation. Indeed, if it were said to him that the sun is about 150 or 160 times greater than the earth, he would count this statement as madness on the part of the one who makes it.[8] And this is something for which a demonstration has been brought forth in astronomy and which no one adept in that science doubts.

(٧) وإذا كان الأمر هكذا وكان كل ما يُحتاج إليه من النظر في أمر المقاييس العقلية قد فحص عنه القدماء أتم فحص، فقد ينبغي أن نضرب بأيدينا إلى كتبهم فننظر فيما قالوه من ذلك، فإن كان كله صوابا قبلناه منهم، وإن كان فيه ما ليس بصواب نبهنا عليه.

(٨) فإذا فرغنا من هذا الجنس من النظر وحصلت عندنا الآلات التي بها نقدر على الاعتبار في الموجودات ودلالة الصنعة فيها – فإن من لا يعرف الصنعة لا يعرف المصنوع ومن لا يعرف المصنوع لا يعرف الصانع – فقد يجب أن نشرع في الفحص عن الموجودات على الترتيب والنحو الذي استفدناه من صناعة المعرفة بالمقاييس البرهانية. وبيّن أيضا أن هذا الغرض إنما يتم لنا في الموجودات بتداول الفحص عنها واحدا بعد واحد وأن يستعين في ذلك المتأخرُ بالمتقدم، على مثال ما عرض في علوم التعاليم.

فإنه لو فرضنا صناعة الهندسة في وقتنا هذا معدومة وكذلك صناعة علم الهيئة، ورام إنسان واحد من تلقاء نفسه أن يدرك مقادير الأجرام السماوية وأشكالها وأبعادها بعضها عن بعض، لما أمكنه ذلك – مثل أن يعرف قدر الشمس من الأرض وغير ذلك من مقادير الكواكب – ولو كان أذكى الناس طبعا، إلا بوحي أو بشيء يشبه الوحي. بل لو قيل له إن الشمس أعظم من الأرض بنحو مائة وخمسين ضعفا أو ستين، لَعُدّ هذا القول جنونا من قائله، وهذا شيء قد قام عليه البرهان في علم الهيئة قياما لا يشك فيه مَن هو مِن أهل ذلك العلم.

There is hardly any need to use an example from the art of mathe-
matics, for reflection upon this art | of the roots of jurisprudence, and
jurisprudence itself, has been perfected only over a long period of time.
If someone today wished to grasp on his own all of the proofs inferred by
5   those in the legal schools who reflect upon the controversial questions
debated[9] in most Islamic countries, even excepting the Maghrib,[10] he
would deserve to be laughed at, because that would be impossible for
him—in addition to having already been done. This is a self-evident
matter, not only with respect to the scientific arts, but also with respect
10   to the practical ones. For there is not an art among them that a single
person can bring about on his own. So how can this be done with the art
of arts—namely, wisdom?[11]

(9) Since this is so, if we find that our predecessors in former nations
have reflected upon existing things and considered them according to
15   what is required by the conditions of demonstration, it is perhaps obligatory for us to reflect upon what they say about that and upon what they
establish in their books. Thus, we will accept, rejoice in, and thank them
for whatever agrees with the truth; and we will alert to, warn against,
and excuse them for whatever does not agree with the truth.

20   (10) From this it has become evident that reflection upon the books
of the Ancients is obligatory according to the Law, for their aim and
intention in their books is the very intention to which the Law urges us.
And [it has become evident] that whoever forbids reflection upon them
by anyone suited to reflect upon them—namely, anyone who unites two
25   qualities, the first being innate intelligence and the second Law-based
justice and moral virtue—surely bars people from the door through which

وما الذي أحوج في هذا إلى التمثيل بصناعة التعاليم وهذه
صناعة [٥] أصول الفقه والفقه نفسه لم يكمل النظر فيها إلا في
زمان طويل، ولو رام أنسان اليوم من تلقاء نفسه أن يقف على
جميع الحجاج التي استنبطها النظار من أهل المذاهب في مسائل
الخلاف التي وُضعت المناظرة فيها بينهم في معظم بلاد الإسلام ما   ٥
عدا المغرب، لكان أهلا أن يُضحَك منه لكون ذلك ممتنعا في حقه
مع وجود ذلك مفروغا منه. وهذا أمر بيّن بنفسه ليس في الصنائع
العلمية فقط بل وفي العملية، فإنه ليس منها صناعة يقدر أن ينشئها
واحد بعينه، فكيف بصناعة الصناعة وهي الحكمة.

(٩) وإذا كان هذا هكذا فقد يجب علينا، إن ألفينا لمن تقدمنا   ١٠
من الأمم السالفة نظرا في الموجودات واعتبارا لها بحسب ما
اقتضته شرائط البرهان، أن ننظر في الذي قالوه من ذلك وما أثبتوه
في كتبهم، فما كان منها موافقا للحق قبلناه منهم وسررنا به
وشكرناهم عليه، وما كان منها غير موافق للحق نبهنا عليه وحذرنا
منه وعذرناهم.   ١٥

(١٠) فقد تبين من هذا أن النظر في كتب القدماء واجب
بالشرع، إذ كان مغزاهم في كتبهم ومقصدهم هو المقصد الذي
حثنا الشرع عليه، وأن من نهى عن النظر فيها من كان أهلا للنظر
فيها – وهو الذي جمع أمرين، أحدهما ذكاء الفطرة والثاني العدالة
الشرعية والفضيلة الخلقية – فقد صد الناس عن الباب الذي دعا   ٢٠

the Law calls them to cognizance of God—namely, the door of reflection leading to true cognizance of Him. That is extreme ignorance and estrangement from God (may He be exalted).

If someone goes astray in reflection and stumbles—due either to a deficiency in his innate disposition, poor ordering of his reflection, being overwhelmed by his passions, not finding a teacher to guide him to an understanding of what is in them, or because of a combination of all or more than one of these reasons—it does not follow that they[12] are to be forbidden to the one | who is suited to reflect upon them. For this manner of harm coming about due to them is something that attaches to them by accident, not by essence. It is not obligatory to renounce something useful in its nature and essence because of something harmful existing in it by accident. That is why he [that is, the Prophet] (peace upon him) said to the one who complained about having been ordered to give his brother honey to drink for his diarrhea—because the diarrhea increased when he was given the honey to drink—"God spoke the truth, whereas your brother's stomach lied."[13]

Indeed, we say that anyone who prevents someone suited to reflect upon the books of wisdom from doing so on the grounds that it is supposed some vicious people became perplexed due to reflecting upon them is like one who prevents thirsty people from drinking cool, fresh water until they die of thirst because some people choked on it and died. For dying by choking on water is an accidental matter, whereas [dying] by thirst is an essential, necessary matter. And what occurred through this art is something accidental, [occurring] through the rest of the arts. To how many jurists has jurisprudence been a cause of diminished devoutness and immersion in this world! Indeed, we find most jurists to be like this, yet what their art requires in essence is practical virtue.

الشرع منه الناس إلى معرفة الله، وهو باب النظر المؤدي إلى معرفته حق المعرفة، وذلك غاية الجهل والبعد عن الله تعالى.

وليس يلزم من أنه، إن غوى غاو بالنظر وزل زال – إما من قِبَل نقص فطرته وإما من قِبَل سوء ترتيب نظره فيها أو من قِبَل غلبة شهواته عليه، أو أنه لم يجد معلما يرشده إلى فهم ما فيها أو من قِبَل اجتماع هذه الأسباب فيه أو أكثر من واحد منها – أن يمنعها عن الذي [٦] هو أهل للنظر فيها. فإن هذا النحو من الضرر الداخل من قِبَلها هو شيء لحقها بالعرض لا بالذات، وليس فيما يجب كان نافعا بطباعه وذاته أن يُترَك لمكان مضرة موجودة فيه بالعرض.

ولذلك قال عليه السلام للذي أمَرَه بسقيْ العسل أخاه لإسهال كان به، فتزيّد الإسهال به لما سقاه العسل، وشكا ذلك إليه، «صدق الله وكذب بطن أخيك».

بل نقول إن مثَل من منع النظر في كتب الحكمة من هو أهل لها من أجل أن قوما من أراذل الناس قد يُظَن بهم أنهم ضلوا من قبل نظرهم فيها، مثَل من منع العطاشى شرب الماء البارد العذب حتى ماتوا من العطش، لأن قوما شرقوا به فماتوا. فإن الموت عن الماء بالشَّرَق أمر عارض وعن العطش أمر ذاتي ضروري. وهذا الذي عرض لهذه الصناعة هو شيء عارض لسائر الصنائع. فكم من فقيه كان الفقه سببا لقلة تورعه وخوضه في الدنيا، بل أكثر الفقهاء كذلك نجدهم، وصناعتهم إنما تقتضي بالذات الفضيلة العملية. فإذًا

Therefore, it is not strange that there occurs, with respect to the art requiring scientific virtue, what occurs with respect to the art requiring practical virtue.

[III. That demonstration accords with the Law]

[A. The Law calls to humans by three methods]

(11) Since all of this has been determined and we, the Muslim community, believe that this divine Law of ours is true and is the one alerting to and calling for this happiness—which is cognizance of God (Mighty and Magnificent) and of His creation—therefore, that is determined for every Muslim in accordance with the method of assent his temperament and nature require.

That is because people's natures vary in excellence with respect to assent. Thus, some assent by means of demonstration; some assent by means of dialectical statements in the same way the one adhering to demonstration assents by means of demonstration, there being nothing greater in their natures; and some assent by means of rhetorical statements, just as the one adhering to demonstration assents by means of demonstrative statements.

That is because, when this divine Law of ours | called to people by means of these three methods, assent to it was extended to every human being—except to the one who denies it obstinately in speech or for whom no methods have been determined in it for summoning to God (may He be exalted) due to his own neglect of that. Therefore, he [that is, the Prophet] (peace upon him) was selected to be sent to "the red and the black"[14]—I mean, because of his Law containing [different] methods of calling to God (may He be exalted). And that is manifest in His statement, "Call to the path of your Lord by wisdom, fine preaching, and arguing with them by means of what is finest" [16:125].

[B. Demonstration does not differ from the Law]

(12) Since this Law is true and calls to the reflection leading to cognizance of the truth, we, the Muslim community, know firmly that demonstrative reflection does not lead to differing with what is set down

لا يبعد أن يعرض في الصناعة التي تقتضي الفضيلة العلمية ما
عرض في الصناعة التي تقتضي الفضيلة العملية.

(١١) وإذا تقرر هذا كله، وكنا نعتقد معشر المسلمين أن شريعتنا
هذه الإلهية حق، وأنها التي نبهت على هذه السعادة ودعت إليها
التي هي المعرفة بالله عز وجل وبمخلوقاته، فإن ذلك متقرر عند كل
مسلم من الطريق الذي اقتضته جبلّته وطبيعته من التصديق.

وذلك أن طباع الناس متفاضلة في التصديق، فمنهم من يصدق
بالبرهان، ومنهم من يصدق بالأقاويل الجدلية تصديق صاحب البرهان
بالبرهان – إذ ليس في طباعه أكثر من ذلك – ومنهم من يصدق
بالأقاويل الخطابية كتصديق صاحب البرهان بالأقاويل البرهانية.

وذلك أنه لما كانت شريعتنا هذه الإلهية قد [٧] دعت الناس من
هذه الطرق الثلاث عمّ التصديق بها لكل إنسان، إلا من جحدها
عنادا بلسانه أو لم تتقرر عنده طرق الدعاء فيها إلى الله تعالى لإغفاله
ذلك من نفسه. ولذلك خُصَّ عليه السلام بالبعث إلى «الأحمر
والأسود» – أعني لتضمن شريعته طرق الدعاء إلى الله تعالى، وذلك
صريح في قوله «ٱدْعُ إِلَىٰ سَبِيلِ رَبِّكَ بِٱلْحِكْمَةِ وَٱلْمَوْعِظَةِ ٱلْحَسَنَةِ
وَجَادِلْهُم بِٱلَّتِي هِيَ أَحْسَنُ» [١٦:١٢٥].

(١٢) وإذا كانت هذه الشريعة حقا وداعية إلى النظر المؤدي
إلى معرفة الحق، فإنا معشر المسلمين نعلم على القطع أنه لا يؤدى

in the Law. For truth does not oppose truth; rather, it agrees with and bears witness to it.

(13) Since this is so, if demonstrative reflection leads to any manner of cognizance about any existing thing, that existing thing cannot escape either being passed over in silence in the Law or being made cognizable in it. If it is passed over in silence, there is no contradiction here; it has the status of the statutes passed over in silence that the jurist infers by means of Law-based syllogistic reasoning. If the Law does pronounce about it, the apparent sense of the pronouncement cannot escape either being in agreement with what demonstration leads to, or being different from it. If it is in agreement, there is no argument here. And, if it is different, that is where an interpretation is pursued. The meaning of interpretation is: drawing out the figurative significance of an utterance from its true significance[15] without violating the custom of the Arabic language with respect to figurative speech in doing so—such as calling a thing by what resembles it, its cause, its consequence, what compares to it, or another of the things enumerated in making the sorts of figurative discourse cognizable.

(14) Since the jurist does this with respect to many of the Law-based statutes, how much more fitting is it for the one adhering to demonstrative science to do so. The jurist has only a syllogism based on supposition, whereas the one who is cognizant has a syllogism based on certainty. And we firmly affirm that, whenever demonstration leads to something differing from the apparent sense of the Law, | that apparent sense admits of interpretation according to the rule of interpretation in Arabic.

No Muslim doubts this proposition, nor is any faithful person suspicious of it. Its certainty has been greatly increased for anyone who has pursued this idea, tested it, and has as an intention this reconciling of what is intellected with what is transmitted. Indeed, we say that whenever the apparent sense of a pronouncement about something in the

النظر البرهاني إلى مخالفة ما ورد به الشرع، فإن الحق لا يضاد الحق بل يوافقه ويشهد له.

(١٣) وإذا كان هذا هكذا، فإن أدى النظر البرهاني إلى نحو ما من المعرفة بموجود ما، فلا يخلو ذلك الموجود أن يكون قد سُكت عنه في الشرع أو عُرّف به. فإن كان مما قد سُكت عنه فلا تعارض هنالك، وهو بمنزلة ما سُكت عنه من الأحكام فاستنبطها الفقيه بالقياس الشرعي. وإن كانت نطقت به الشريعة، فلا يخلو ظاهر النطق أن يكون موافقا لما أدى إليه البرهان أو مخالفا. فإن كان موافقا فلا قول هنالك. وإن كان مخالفا طُلب هنالك تأويله. ومعنى التأويل هو إخراج دلالة اللفظ من الدلالة الحقيقية إلى الدلالة المجازية ‒ من غير أن يُخِل في ذلك بعادة لسان العرب في التجوّز ‒ من تسمية الشيء بشبيهه أو بسببه أو لاحقه أو مُقَارنه أو غير ذلك من الأشياء التي عُددت في تعريف أصناف الكلام المجازي.

(١٤) وإذا كان الفقيه يفعل هذا في كثير من الأحكام الشرعية، فكم بالحريّ أن يفعل ذلك صاحب علم البرهان. فإن الفقيه إنما عنده قياس ظني والعارف قياس يقيني. ونحن نقطع قطعا أن كل ما أدى إليه البرهان وخالفه ظاهر الشرع أن [٨] ذلك الظاهر يقبل التأويل على قانون التأويل العربي.

وهذه القضية لا يشك فيها مسلم ولا يرتاب بها مؤمن، وما أعظم ازدياد اليقين بها عند من زاول هذا المعنى وجربه وقصد هذا المقصد من الجمع بين المعقول والمنقول. بل نقول إنه ما من منطوق

Law differs from what demonstration leads to, if the Law is considered and all of its parts scrutinized, there will invariably be found in the utterances of the Law something whose apparent sense bears witness, or comes close to bearing witness, to that interpretation.

5   Because of this idea, Muslims have formed a consensus[16] that it is not obligatory for all the utterances of the Law to be taken in their apparent sense, nor for all of them to be drawn out from their apparent sense by means of interpretation, though they disagree about which ones are to be interpreted and which not interpreted. The Ashᶜarites,[17] for
10   example, interpret the verse about God's directing Himself [2:29] and the Tradition about His descent,[18] whereas the Ḥanbalites[19] take them in their apparent sense.

The reason an apparent and an inner sense are set down in the Law is the difference in people's innate dispositions and the variance in their
15   innate capacities for assent. The reason contradictory apparent senses are set down in it is to alert "those well grounded in science" to the interpretation that reconciles them. This idea is pointed to in His statement (may He be exalted), "He it is who has sent down to you the Book; in it, there are fixed verses . . ." on to His statement, "and those well grounded
20   in science" [3:7].[20]

(15) If someone were to say: "Muslims have formed a consensus that in the Law are things to be taken in their apparent sense and things to be interpreted, and there are things about which they disagree. So, is it permissible for demonstration to lead to interpreting what they have
25   formed a consensus to take in its apparent sense, or to taking in its apparent sense what they have formed a consensus to interpret?" we would say: "If the consensus were established by a method of certainty, it would not be valid [to do so]; but if the consensus about them were suppositional, then it would be valid [to do so]." That is why Abū Ḥāmid
30   [al-Ghazālī], Abū al-Maᶜālī,[21] and others from among the leading thinkers[22] said that unbelief is to be affirmed of no one for going against consensus by interpreting things like these.

به في الشرع مخالف بظاهره لما أدى إليه البرهان، إلا إذا اعتُبر الشرع وتُصفِّحت سائر أجزائه وجد في ألفاظ الشرع ما يشهد بظاهره لذلك التأويل أو يقارب أن يشهد.

ولهذا المعنى أجمع المسلمون على أنه ليس يجب أن تُحمَل ألفاظ الشرع كلها على ظاهرها ولا أن تُخرَج كلها عن ظاهرها بالتأويل، واختلفوا في المؤوَّل منها من غير المؤوَّل، فالأشعريون مثلا يتأوّلون آية الاستواء [٢٩:٢] وحديث النزول، والحنابلة تحمل ذلك على ظاهره.

والسبب في ورود الشرع فيه الظاهر والباطن هو اختلاف فِطَر الناس وتباين قرائحهم في التصديق، والسبب في ورود الظواهر المتعارضة فيه هو تنبيه الراسخين في العلم على التأويل الجامع بينها. وإلى هذا المعنى وردت الإشارة بقوله تعالى ﴿هُوَ ٱلَّذِى أَنزَلَ عَلَيْكَ ٱلْكِتَابَ مِنْهُ آيَاتٌ مُّحْكَمَاتٌ...﴾ إلى قوله ﴿وَٱلرَّاسِخُونَ فِى ٱلْعِلْمِ﴾ [٧:٣].

(١٥) فإن قال قائل: فإن في الشرع أشياء قد أجمع المسلمون على حملها على ظواهرها وأشياء على تأويلها وأشياء اختلفوا فيها، فهل يجوز أن يؤدي البرهان إلى تأويل ما أجمعوا على ظاهره أو ظاهر ما أجمعوا على تأويله. قلنا: أما لو ثبت الإجماع بطريق يقيني لم يصح، وأما إن كان الإجماع فيها ظنيا فقد يصح، ولذلك قال أبو حامد وأبو المعالي وغيرهما من أئمة النظر إنه لا يُقطَع بكفر من خرق الإجماع في التأويل في أمثال هذه الأشياء.

What may indicate to you that consensus is not to be determined
with certainty about theoretical matters,[23] as it is possible for it to be
determined about practical matters, is that it is not possible | for consen-
sus to be determined about a particular question at a particular epoch
unless: that epoch is delimited by us; all the learned men existing in that
epoch are known to us, I mean, known as individuals and in their total
number; the doctrine of each one of them on the question is transmitted
to us by means of an uninterrupted transmission;[24] and, in addition to all
this, it has been certified to us that the learned men existing at that time
agreed that there is not an apparent and an inner sense to the Law, that it
is obligatory that knowledge of every question be concealed from no one,
and that there is only one method for people to know the Law.

It has been transmitted that many in the earliest days [of Islam] used
to be of the opinion that the Law has both an apparent and an inner
sense and that it is not obligatory for someone to know about the inner
sense if he is not an adept in knowledge of it nor capable of understanding it. There is, for example, what al-Bukhārī relates about ᶜAlī ibn Abū
Ṭālib (may God be pleased with him), saying, "Speak to the people concerning what they are cognizant of. Do you want God and His messenger
to be accused of lying?"[25] And there is, for example, what is related of
that about a group of the early followers [of Islam]. So how is it possible
to conceive of consensus about a single theoretical question being transmitted to us when we firmly know that no single epoch has escaped having learned men who are of the opinion that there are things in the Law
not all of the people ought to know in their true sense? That differs from
what occurs with practical matters, for everybody is of the opinion that
they are to be disclosed to all people alike; and, for consensus about
them to be reached, we deem it sufficient that the question be widely
diffused and that no difference [of opinion] about it be transmitted to us.

وقد يدلك على أن الإجماع لا يتقرر في النظريات بطريق يقيني كما يمكن أن يتقرر في العمليات، أنه ليس يمكن [٩] أن يتقرر الإجماع في مسألة ما في عصر ما إلا بأن يكون ذلك العصر عندنا محصورا وأن يكون جميع العلماء الموجودين في ذلك العصر

٥ معلومين عندنا – أعني معلوما أشخاصهم ومبلغ عددهم – وأن يُنقَل إلينا في المسألة مذهب كل واحد منهم نقل تواتر، ويكون مع هذا كله قد صح عندنا أن العلماء الموجودين في ذلك الزمان متفقون على أنه ليس في الشرع ظاهر وباطن وأن العلم بكل مسألة يجب أن لا يُكتَم عن أحد وأن الناس طريقهم واحد في علم الشريعة.

١٠ وأما وكثير من الصدر الأول قد نُقل عنهم أنهم كانوا يرون أن للشرع ظاهرا وباطنا وأنه ليس يجب أن يعلم بالباطن من ليس من أهل العلم به ولا يقدر على فهمه – مثل ما روى البخاري عن علي بن أبي طالب رضي الله عنه أنه قال: ((حدثوا الناس بما يعرفون، أتريدون أن يُكذَّب الله ورسوله))، ومثل ما رُوي من ذلك عن

١٥ جماعة من السلف – فكيف يمكن أن يُتصَّور إجماع منقول إلينا عن مسألة من المسائل النظرية ونحن نعلم قطعا أنه لا يخلو عصر من الأعصار من علماء يرون أن في الشرع أشياء لا ينبغي أن يعلم بحقيقتها جميع الناس. وذلك بخلاف ما عرض في العمليات، فإن الناس كلهم يرون إفشاءها لجميع الناس على السواء، ونكتفي

٢٠ بحصول الإجماع فيها بأن لا تنتشر المسألة فلا يُنقَل إلينا فيها

Now, this is sufficient for reaching consensus about practical matters;
but the case with scientific matters is different.

[C. Whether the philosophers are guilty of unbelief]

(16) If you were to say: "If it is not obligatory to charge with unbelief
one who goes against consensus with respect to interpretation, since con-
5   sensus with respect to that is not conceivable, what do you say about the
philosophers among the adherents of Islam like Abū Naṣr [al-Fārābī]
and Ibn Sīnā [Avicenna]? For in his book known as *The Incoherence [of the
Philosophers]*, Abū Ḥāmid [al-Ghazālī] has firmly charged both of them as
unbelievers with respect to three questions: the argument about the
10   eternity of the world, that the Exalted does not know particulars—may
He be exalted above that—and | the interpretation of what is set forth
about the resurrection of bodies and the way things are in the next
life,"26 we would say: "The apparent sense of what he says about that is
that he does not firmly charge them with unbelief about that, for he has
15   declared in the book *The Distinction* that charging someone with unbelief
for going against consensus is tentative.27 And it has become evident
from our argument that it is not possible for consensus to be determined
with respect to questions like these because of what is related about
many of the first followers [of Islam], as well as others, holding that
20   there are interpretations that it is not obligatory to expound except to
those adept in interpretation."

These are "those well grounded in science"—for we choose to place
the stop after His statement (may He be exalted), "and those well grounded
in science" [3:7].28 Now, if those adept in science did not know the inter-
25   pretation, there would be nothing superior in their assent obliging them
to a faith in Him not found among those not adept in science. Yet God has
already described them as those who have faith in Him, and this refers
only to faith coming about from demonstration. And it comes about only
along with the science of interpretation.

خلاف. فإن هذا كاف في حصول الإجماع في العمليات بخلاف الأمر في العلميات.

(١٦) فإن قلت: فإذا لم يجب التكفير بخرق الإجماع في التأويل إذ لا يُتصوَّر في ذلك إجماع، فما تقول في الفلاسفة من أهل الإسلام كأبي نصر وابن سينا، فإن أبا حامد قد قطع بتكفيرهما في كتابه المعروف بـ((التهافت)) في ثلاث مسائل: في القول بقدم العالم وبأنه تعالى لا يعلم الجزئيات – تعالى عن ذلك – وفي [١٠] تأويل ما جاء في حشر الأجساد وأحوال المعاد. قلنا: الظاهر من قوله في ذلك أنه ليس تكفيره إياهما في ذلك قطعا، إذ قد صرح في كتاب ((التفرقة)) أن التكفير بخرق الإجماع فيه احتمال. وقد تبين من قولنا أنه ليس يمكن أن يتقرر إجماع في أمثال هذه المسائل، لما رُوي عن كثير من السلف الأول فضلا عن غيرهم أن ههنا تأويلات لا يجب أن يُفصَح بها إلا لمن هو من أهل التأويل.

وهم الراسخون في العلم – لأن الاختيار عندنا هو الوقوف على قوله تعالى ((وَالرَّاسِخُونَ فِى ٱلْعِلْمِ)) [٧:٣]. لأنه إذا لم يكن أهل العلم يعلمون التأويل لم تكن عندهم مزية تصديق توجب لهم من الإيمان به ما لا يوجد عند غير أهل العلم. وقد وصفهم الله بأنهم المؤمنون به، وهذا إنما يُحمَل على الإيمان الذي يكون من قبل البرهان، وهذا لا يكون إلا مع العلم بالتأويل.

Those faithful not adept in science are people whose faith in them[29] is not based on demonstration. So, if this faith by which God has described the learned is particular to them, then it is obligatory that it come about by means of demonstration. And if it is by means of demonstration, then it comes about only along with the science of interpretation. For God (may He be exalted) has already announced that there is an interpretation of them that is the truth, and demonstration is only of the truth. Since that is the case, it is not possible for an exhaustive consensus to be determined with respect to the interpretations by which God particularly characterized the learned. This is self-evident to anyone who is fair-minded.

(17) In addition to all of this, we are of the opinion that Abū Ḥāmid [al-Ghazālī] was mistaken about the Peripatetic sages when he accused them of saying that He (Holy and Exalted) does not know particulars at all. Rather, they are of the opinion that He knows them (may He be exalted) by means of a knowledge that is not of the same kind as our knowledge of them. That is because our knowledge of them is an effect of what is known, so that it is generated when the known thing is generated and changes when it changes. And the knowledge God (glorious is He) has of existence is the opposite of this: it is the cause of the thing known, which is the existing thing.

So, whoever likens | the two kinds of knowledge to one another sets down two opposite essences and their particular characteristics as being one, and that is the extreme of ignorance. If the name "knowledge" is said of knowledge that is generated and of knowledge that is eternal, it is said purely as a name that is shared, just as many names are said of opposite things—for example, *al-jalal,* said of great and small, and *al-ṣarīm,* said of light and darkness.[30] Thus, there is no definition embracing both kinds of knowledge, as the dialectical theologians of our time fancy.

Prompted by one of our friends, we have devoted a statement to this question.[31] How is it to be fancied that the Peripatetics would say that He (glorious is He) does not know particulars with eternal knowledge,

فإن غير أهل العلم من المؤمنين هم أهل الإيمان بها لا من قِبَل البرهان، فإن كان هذا الإيمان الذي وصف الله به العلماء خاصا بهم فيجب أن يكون بالبرهان، وإن كان بالبرهان فلا يكون إلا مع علم التأويل، لأن الله تعالى قد أخبر أن لها تأويلا هو الحقيقة، والبرهان لا يكون إلا على الحقيقة. وإذا كان ذلك كذلك فلا يمكن أن يتقرر في التأويلات التي خص الله العلماء بها إجماع مستفيض، وهذا بيّن بنفسه عند من أنصف.

(١٧) وإلى هذا كله فقد نرى أن أبا حامد قد غلط على الحكماء المشائين فيما نسب اليهم من أنهم يقولون إنه تقدس وتعالى لا يعلم الجزئيات أصلا، بل يرون أنه يعلمها تعالى بعلم غير مجانس لعلمنا بها. وذلك أن علمنا بها معلول للمعلوم به فهو محدَث بحدوثه ومتغير بتغيره، وعلم الله سبحانه في الوجود على مقابل هذا فإنه علة للمعلوم الذي هو الموجود.

فمن شبّه [١١] العلمين أحدهما بالآخر فقد جعل ذوات المتقابلات وخواصها واحدة وذلك غاية الجهل. فاسم العلم إذا قيل على العلم المحدَث والقديم فهو مقول باشتراك الإسم المحض كما يقال كثير من الأسماء على المتقابلات – مثل «الجَلَل» المقول على العظيم والصغير و«الصريم» المقول على الضوء والظلمة. ولهذا ليس ههنا حد يشتمل العلمين جميعا كما توهمه المتكلمون من أهل زماننا.

وقد أفردنا في هذه المسألة قولا حركنا إليه بعض أصحابنا. وكيف يُتوهَّم على المشائين أنهم يقولون أنه سبحانه لا يعلم بالعلم

when they are of the opinion that true dream-visions contain premoni-
tions of particular things that are to be generated in the future and that
this premonitional knowledge reaches human beings in sleep due to the
everlasting knowledge governing the whole and having mastery over it?
5   Moreover, it is not only particulars that they are of the opinion He does
not know in the way we know them, but universals as well. For, the universals known to us are also effects of the nature of the existing thing,
whereas, with that knowledge [of His], it is the reverse. Therefore, that
knowledge [of His] has been demonstrated to transcend description as
10 "universal" or "particular." So there is no reason for disagreement about
this question—I mean, about charging them with unbelief or not charging them with unbelief.

(18) As for the question whether the world is eternal or has been generated, the disagreement between the Ashʿarite dialectical theologians
15 and the ancient sages almost comes back, in my view, to a disagreement
about naming, especially with respect to some of the Ancients. That is
because they agree that there are three sorts of existing things: two
extremes and one intermediate between the extremes. And they agree
about naming the two extremes but disagree about the intermediate.
20 One extreme is an existent thing that exists from something other
than itself and by something—I mean, by an agent cause[32] and from
matter. And time precedes it—I mean, its existence. This is the case of
bodies whose coming into being is apprehended | by sense perception—
for example, the coming into being of water, air, earth, animals, plants,
25 and so forth. The Ancients and the Ashʿarites both agree in naming this
sort of existing things "generated."

القديم الجزئيات، وهم يرون أن الرؤيا الصادقة تتضمن الإنذارات
بالجزئيات الحادثة في الزمان المستقبل وأن ذلك العلم المنذر يحصل
للإنسان في النوم من قِبَل العلم الأزلي المدبر للكل والمستولي عليه.
وليس يرون أنه لا يعلم الجزئيات فقط على النحو الذي نعلمه نحن
بل ولا الكليات، فإن الكليات المعلومة عندنا معلولة أيضا عن
طبيعة الموجود والأمر في ذلك العلم بالعكس. ولذلك ما قد أدى
إليه البرهان أن ذلك العلم منزَّه عن أن يوصَف بـ«كلي» أو
بـ«جزئي»، فلا معنى للإختلاف في هذه المسألة – أعني في
تكفيرهم أو لا تكفيرهم.

(١٨) وأما مسألة قدم العالم أو حدوثه فإن الاختلاف فيها
عندي بين المتكلمين من الأشعرية وبين الحكماء المتقدمين يكاد
يكون راجعا للإختلاف في التسمية وبخاصة عند بعض القدماء.
وذلك أنهم اتفقوا على أن ههنا ثلاثة أصناف من الموجودات،
طرفان وواسطة بين الطرفين. فاتفقوا في تسمية الطرفين واختلفوا
في الواسطة.

فأما الطرف الواحد فهو موجود وجد من شيء غيره وعن
شيء، أعني عن سبب فاعل ومن مادة، والزمان متقدم عليه، أعني
على وجوده. وهذه هي حال الأجسام التي يُدرَك تكوّنها [١٢]
بالحس – مثل تكوّن الماء والهواء والأرض والحيوان والنبات وغير
ذلك. وهذا الصنف من الموجودات اتفق الجميع من القدماء
والأشعريين على تسميتها «محدَثة».

The extreme opposed to this is an existent thing that has not come
into existence from something or by something and that time does not
precede. About this, too, both factions agree in naming it "eternal." This
existent thing is apprehended by demonstration: it is God (may He be
5   blessed and exalted) who is the Agent[33] of the whole, its Giver of Existence, and its Sustainer (glorious is He, and may His might be exalted).

The sort of being between these two extremes is an existent thing
that has not come into existence from something and that time does not
precede, but that does come into existence by something—I mean, by an
10   agent. This is the world as a whole.

Now, all of them agree on the existence of these three attributes with
respect to the world. For, the dialectical theologians admit that time does
not precede it—or, rather, that is a consequence of their holding that
time is something joined to motions and bodies. They also agree with the
15   Ancients about future time being infinite and, likewise, future existence.
And they disagree only about past time and past existence. For the
dialectical theologians are of the opinion that it is limited, which is the
doctrine of Plato and his sect, while Aristotle and his faction are of
the opinion that it is infinite, as is the case with the future.

20   (19) So it is evident that this latter existent thing has been taken as
resembling the existing thing that truly comes into being and the eternally existing thing. Those overwhelmed by its resemblance to the eternal
rather than to what is generated name it "eternal," and those overwhelmed
by its resemblance to what is generated name it "generated." But, in
25   truth, it is not truly generated, nor is it truly eternal. For what is truly
generated is necessarily corruptible, and what is truly eternal has no
cause. Among them are those who name it "everlastingly generated"—
namely, Plato and his sect, because time according to them is finite with
respect to the past.

وأما الطرف المقابل لهذا فهو موجود لم يكن من شيء ولا عن شيء ولا تقدمه زمان، وهذا أيضا اتفق الجميع من الفرقتين على تسميته «قديما». وهذا الموجود مدرَك بالبرهان وهو الله تبارك وتعالى الذي هو فاعل الكل وموجده والحافظ له سبحانه وتعالى قدره.

وأما الصنف من الموجود الذي بين هذين الطرفين فهو موجود لم يكن من شيء ولا تقدمه زمان ولكنه موجود عن شيء، أعني عن فاعل، وهذا هو العالم بأسره.

والكل منهم متفق على وجود هذه الصفات الثلاث للعالم. فإن المتكلمين يسلمون أن الزمان غير متقدم عليه – أو يلزمهم ذلك إذ الزمان عندهم شيء مقارن للحركات والأجسام. وهم أيضا متفقون مع القدماء على أن الزمان المستقبل غير متناه وكذلك الوجود المستقبل. وإنما يختلفون في الزمان الماضي والوجود الماضي. فالمتكلمون يرون أنه متناه، وهذا هو مذهب أفلاطون وشيعته، وأرسطو وفرقته يرون أنه غير متناه كالحال في المستقبل.

(١٩) فهذا الوجود الآخرالأمر فيه بيّن أنه قد أخذ شبها من الوجود الكائن الحقيقي ومن الوجود القديم. فمن غلب عليه ما فيه من شبه القديم على ما فيه من شبه المحدَث سماه «قديما»، ومن غلب عليه ما فيه من شبه المحدَث سماه «محدَثا» وهو في الحقيقة ليس محدَثا حقيقيا ولا قديما حقيقيا، فإن المحدَث الحقيقي فاسد ضرورة والقديم الحقيقي ليس له علة. ومنهم من سماه «محدَثا أزليا» – وهو أفلاطون وشيعته – لكون الزمان متناهيا عندهم من الماضي.

(20) Thus, the doctrines about the world are not all so far apart from one another that some of them should be charged as unbelief and others not. Indeed, for opinions | to be such that this should happen, it is obligatory that they be excessively far apart—I mean, that they be opposites of each other, as the dialectical theologians suppose they are with respect to this question—that is, that the name "eternity" and that of "generated" with respect to the world as a whole are opposites of each other. And it has already become evident from our statement that the matter is not like that.

(21) In addition to all this, these opinions about the world do not conform to the apparent sense of the Law. For if the apparent sense of the Law is scrutinized, it will become apparent from the verses comprising a communication about the coming into existence of the world that, in truth, its form is generated, whereas being itself and time extend continuously at both extremes—I mean, without interruption. That is because His statement (may He be exalted), "And He is the one Who created the heavens and the earth in six days, and His throne was on the water" [11:7], requires, in its apparent sense, an existence before this existence—namely, the throne and water—and a time before this time, I mean, the one joined to the form of this existence, which is the number of the movement of the heavenly sphere. And His statement (may He be exalted), "On the day the earth shall be changed into other than earth, and the heavens also" [14:48], in its apparent sense also requires a second existence after this existence. And His statement (may He be exalted), "Then He directed Himself toward the heaven, and it was smoke" [41:11], requires in its apparent sense that the heavens were created from something.

(22) Nor do the dialectical theologians conform to the apparent sense of the Law in what they say about the world, but interpret it. For it is not [said] in the Law that God was existing along with sheer nothingness; no text whatever to this effect is to be found. So how is it to be conceived that the dialectical theologians' interpretation of these verses would meet with consensus when the apparent sense of the Law with respect to the existence of the world, which we have stated, has already been stated by a faction among the sages?

(٢٠) فالمذاهب في العالم ليس تتباعد كل التباعد حتى يكفِّر بعضها ولا يكفِّر. فإن الآراء[١٣] التي شأنها هذا يجب أن تكون في الغاية من التباعد، أعني أن تكون متقابلة، كما ظن المتكلمون في هذه المسألة، أعني أن اسم ((القدم)) و ((الحدوث)) في العالم بأسره هو من المتقابلة. وقد تبيّن من قولنا أن الأمر ليس كذلك.

(٢١) وهذا كله مع أن هذه الآراء في العالم ليست على ظاهر الشرع، فإن ظاهر الشرع إذا تُصُفِّح ظهر من الآيات الواردة في الإنباء عن إيجاد العالم أن صورته محدَثة بالحقيقة وأن نفس الوجود والزمان مستمر من الطرفين، أعني غير منقطع. وذلك أن قوله تعالى ((وَهُوَ ٱلَّذِى خَلَقَ ٱلسَّمَوَاتِ وَٱلْأَرْضَ فِى سِتَّةِ أَيَّامٍ وَكَانَ عَرْشُهُ عَلَى ٱلْمَآءِ)) [٧:١١] يقتضي بظاهره أن وجودا قبل هذا الوجود وهو العرش والماء وزمانا قبل هذا الزمان اعني المقترن بصورة هذا الوجود الذي هو عد حركة الفلك. وقوله تعالى ((يَوْمَ تُبَدَّلُ ٱلْأَرْضُ غَيْرَ ٱلْأَرْضِ وَٱلسَّمَوَاتُ)) [٤٨:١٤] يقتضي أيضا بظاهره أن وجودا ثانيا بعد هذا الوجود. وقوله تعالى ((ثُمَّ ٱسْتَوَى إِلَى ٱلسَّمَآءِ وَهِيَ دُخَانٌ)) [١١:٤١] يقتضي بظاهره أن السموات خُلقت من شيء.

(٢٢) فالمتكلمون ليسوا في قولهم أيضا في العالم على ظاهر الشرع بل متأولون. فإنه ليس في الشرع أن الله كان موجودا مع العدم المحض، ولا يوجد هذا فيه نصا أبدا. فكيف يُتصَّور في تأويل المتكلمين في هذه الآيات أن الإجماع انعقد عليه، والظاهر الذي قلناه من الشرع في وجود العالم قد قال به فرقة من الحكماء.

(23) It seems that those who disagree about the interpretation of these recondite questions have either hit the mark and are to be rewarded or have erred and are to be excused. For assent to something due to an indication arising in the soul is compulsory, not voluntary—I mean that it is not up to us not to assent or to assent as it is up to us to stand up or not to stand up. Since a condition of responsibility is having choice, the one who assents to error because of vagueness occurring in it is excused if he is an adept of science. | Therefore, he [that is, the Prophet] said (peace upon him), "If the judge hits the mark after exerting himself, he will be rewarded twofold; and if he errs, he will have a single reward."

Now what judge is greater than the one who makes judgments about existence, as to whether it is thus or not thus? These judges are the learned ones whom God has selected for interpretation, and this error that is forgiven according to the Law is only the error occasioned by learned men when they reflect upon the recondite things that the Law makes them responsible for reflecting upon.

(24) The error occasioned by any other sort of people is sheer sin, whether it is an error about theoretical or practical matters. Just as the judge who is ignorant of Tradition[34] is not excused when he errs about a judgment, neither is the judge about existing things in whom the conditions for judgment do not exist excused; indeed, he is either a sinner or an unbeliever. And if it is stipulated, with respect to the judge about what is allowed and what is proscribed, that he combine within himself the reasons for exercising personal judgment[35]—namely, cognizance of the roots and cognizance of what is inferred from these roots by means of syllogistic reasoning—then how much more fitting is it for this to be stipulated with respect to the one who is to judge about existing things, I mean, that he be cognizant of the primary intellectual notions and how to infer from them.

(٢٣) ويشبه أن يكون المختلفون في تأويل هذه المسائل العويصة إما مصيبين مأجورين وإما مخطئين معذورين. فإن التصديق بالشيء من قِبَل الدليل القائم في النفس هو شيء اضطراري لا اختياري، أعني أنه ليس لنا أن لا نصدق أو نصدق كما لنا أن نقوم أو لا نقوم.

٥ وإذا كان من شرط التكليف الاختيار، فالمصدق بالخطأ من قبل شبهة عرضت له إذا كان من أهل العلم معذور. [١٤] ولذلك قال عليه السلام ((إذا اجتهد الحاكم فأصاب فله أجران وإذا أخطأ فله أجر)).

وأي حاكم أعظم من الذي يحكم على الوجود بأنه كذا أو ليس بكذا. وهؤلاء الحكام هم العلماء الذين خصهم الله بالتأويل، وهذا الخطأ المصفوح عنه في الشرع إنما هو الخطأ الذي يقع من العلماء إذا

١٠ نظروا في الأشياء العويصة التي كلفهم الشرع النظر فيها.

(٢٤) وأما الخطأ الذي يقع من غير هذا الصنف من الناس فهو إثم محض، وسواء كان الخطأ في الأمور النظرية أو العملية. فكما أن الحاكم الجاهل بالسنة إذا أخطأ في الحكم لم يكن معذورا، كذلك

١٥ الحاكم على الموجودات إذا لم توجد فيه شروط الحكم فليس بمعذور بل هو إما آثم وإما كافر. وإذا كان يُشترَط في الحاكم في الحلال والحرام أن تجتمع له أسباب الاجتهاد – وهو معرفة الأصول ومعرفة الاستنباط من تلك الأصول بالقياس – فكم بالحري أن يُشترَط ذلك في الحاكم على الموجودات، أعني أن يعرف الأوائل

٢٠ العقلية ووجه الاستنباط منها.

(25) In general, error with respect to the Law is of two types:

There is error that is excused for one who is adept in reflection about that thing concerning which error occurs, just as the skillful physician is excused if he errs with respect to the art of medicine and the skillful judge if he errs with respect to a judgment. But one who is not adept in that concern is not excused.

And there is error that is not excused for anyone whosoever. Rather, it is unbelief if it occurs with respect to the principles of the Law and heretical innovation if it occurs with respect to what is subordinate to the principles.

(26) This error is the very one that comes about concerning the things that all the sorts of methods of indications steer to cognizance of. Thus, cognizance of that thing is, in this manner, possible for everyone. Such, for example, is affirmation of [the existence of] God (may He be blessed and exalted); of the prophetic missions; and of happiness in the hereafter and misery in the hereafter. That is because the three sorts of indications | due to which no one is exempted from assenting to what he is responsible for being cognizant of—I mean, the rhetorical, dialectical, and demonstrative indications—lead to these three roots.

So the one who denies things like these, when they are one of the roots of the Law, is an unbeliever who resists obstinately with his tongue but not his heart, or [who resists obstinately] due to his neglecting to expose himself to cognizance of what indicates them. For if he is an adept of demonstration, a path to assenting to them has been placed before him by demonstration; and if he is an adept of dialectic, then by dialectic; and if he is an adept of preaching, then by preaching. Therefore, he [the Prophet] (peace upon him) said, "I was ordered to combat people until they say, 'There is no god but God,' and have faith in me"— he means by whatever one of the three methods of bringing about faith that suits them.

(٢٥) وبالجملة فالخطأ في الشرع على ضربين:

إما خطأ يُعذَر فيه من هو من أهل النظر في ذلك الشيء الذي وقع فيه الخطأ – كما يُعذَر الطبيب الماهر إذا أخطأ في صناعة الطب والحاكم الماهر إذا أخطأ في الحكم – ولا يُعذَر فيه من ليس من أهل ذلك الشأن.

وإما خطأ ليس يُعذَر فيه أحد من الناس، بل إن وقع في مبادىء الشريعة فهو كفر وإن وقع فيما بعد المبادىء فهو بدعة.

(٢٦) وهذا الخطأ هو الخطأ الذي يكون في الأشياء التي تفضي جميع أصناف طرق الدلائل إلى معرفتها فتكون معرفة ذلك الشيء بهذه الجهة ممكنة للجميع. وهذا هو مثل الإقرار بالله تبارك وتعالى وبالنبوات وبالسعادة الأخراوية والشقاء الأخراوي، وذلك أن هذه الأصول الثلاثة تؤدي إليها أصناف الدلائل الثلاثة التي[١٥] لا يعرى أحد من الناس عن وقوع التصديق له من قبلها بالذي كُلِّف معرفته، أعني الدلائل الخطابية والجدلية والبرهانية.

فالجاحد لأمثال هذه الأشياء إذا كانت أصلاً من أصول الشرع كافر معاند بلسانه دون قلبه أو بغفلته عن التعرض إلى معرفة دليلها، لأنه إن كان من أهل البرهان فقد جُعل له سبيل إلى التصديق بها بالبرهان، وإن كان من أهل الجدل فبالجدل، وإن كان من أهل الموعظة فبالموعظة. ولذلك قال عليه السلام «أمرت أن أقاتل الناس حتى يقولوا لا إله إلا الله ويؤمنوا بي» – يريد بأي طريق اتفق لهم من طرق الإيمان الثلاث.

(27) Concerning the things that are known only by demonstration due to their being hidden, God has been gracious to His servants for whom there is no path by means of demonstration—either due to their innate dispositions, their habits, or their lack of facilities[36] for education—by coining for them likenesses and similarities of these [hidden things] and calling them to assent by means of those likenesses, since it is possible for assent to those likenesses to come about by means of the indications shared by all—I mean, the dialectical and the rhetorical. This is the reason for the Law being divided into an apparent sense and an inner sense. For the apparent sense is those likenesses coined for those meanings, and the inner sense is those meanings that reveal themselves only to those adept in demonstration. These [likenesses and meanings] are the four or five sorts of existing things that Abū Ḥāmid [al-Ghazālī] mentioned in the book *The Distinction*.[37]

(28) If it happens, as we have said, that we know something in itself by means of the three methods, there is no need for us to coin a likeness for it; and, as long as it is in its apparent sense, it does not admit of interpretation. If this manner of apparent sense refers to the roots [of the Law], the one who interprets it would be an unbeliever—like someone believing that there is no happiness or misery in the hereafter and that such a statement is intended only to safeguard people from one another in what pertains to their bodies and physical senses, that it is a stratagem, and that a human being has no end other than sensual existence.

(29) If this has been determined for you, | then it is apparent to you from our statement that there is an apparent sense of the Law that it is not permissible to interpret. To interpret it is unbelief when it has to do with principles and heretical innovation when it has to do with what is subordinate to principles. There is also an apparent sense that it is obligatory for those adept in demonstration to interpret, it being unbelief for them to take it in its apparent sense. Yet for those not adept in demonstration to interpret it and draw it away from its apparent sense is unbelief or heretical innovation on their part.

(٢٧) وأما الأشياء التي لخفائها لا تُعلَم إلا بالبرهان فقد تلطف
الله فيها لعباده الذين لا سبيل لهم إلى البرهان، إما من قبل فطرهم
وإما من قبل عادتهم وإما من قبل عدمهم أسباب التعلم، بأن ضرب
لهم أمثالها وأشباهها ودعاهم إلى التصديف بتلك الأمثال، إذ
كانت تلك الأمثال يمكن أن يقع التصديق بها بالأدلة المشتركة
للجميع، أعني الجدلية والخطابية. وهذا هو السبب في أن انقسم
الشرع إلى ظاهر وباطن، فإن الظاهر هو تلك الأمثال المضروبة
لتلك المعاني، والباطن هو تلك المعاني التي لا تنجلي إلا لأهل
البرهان. وهذه هي أصناف تلك الموجودات الأربعة أو الخمسة
التي ذكرها أبو حامد في كتاب «التفرقة».

(٢٨) وإذا اتفق – كما قلنا – أن نعلم الشيء بنفسه بالطرق
الثلاث، لم نحتج أن نضرب له مثالا وكان على ظاهره لا يتطرق إليه
تأويل. وهذا النحو من الظاهر إن كان في الأصول فالمتأول له كافر،
مثل من يعتقد أنه لا سعادة أخراوية ههنا ولا شقاء وأنه إنما قُصد
بهذا القول أن يسلم الناس بعضهم من بعض في أبدانهم وحواسهم
وأنها حيلة وأنه لا غاية للإنسان إلا وجوده المحسوس فقط.

(٢٩) وإذا تقرر لك هذا [١٦] فقد ظهر لك من قولنا أن ههنا
ظاهرا من الشرع لا يجوز تأويله، فإن كان تأويله في المبادىء فهو
كفر وإن كان فيما بعد المبادىء فهو بدعة، وههنا أيضا ظاهر يجب
على أهل البرهان تأويله، وحملهم إياه على ظاهره كفر، وتأويل
غير أهل البرهان له وإخراجه عن ظاهره كفر في حقهم أو بدعة.

(30) Of this sort is the verse about God's directing Himself [2:29] and the Tradition about His descent.[38] Therefore, he [the Prophet] said (peace upon him) with respect to the black woman, when she announced that God was in heaven: "Set her free, for she is one of the faithful." For she was not one of those adept in demonstration. The reason for that is that for the sort of people who come to assent only due to the imagination—I mean, those who assent to something only insofar as they can imagine it—it is difficult to come to assent to an existing thing that is not linked with something imaginable.

This also applies to those who understand the link only as [God hav-ing] a place—they are the ones who in their reflection have moved some-what beyond the rank of the first sort's belief in corporeality. Therefore, the answer to these people about verses and Traditions like these is that they pertain to the verses that resemble one another and that the stop is at His saying (may He be exalted), "None knows their interpretation but God" [3:7].[39] Even though there is consensus among the people of demonstration that this sort admits of interpretation, they disagree about its interpretation. And that is according to each one's rank with respect to cognizance of demonstration.

(31) There is a third sort [of verses and Traditions] with respect to the Law, one wavering between these [other] two sorts and about which there is doubt. One group of those who occupy themselves with reflection attach this sort to the apparent sense that it is not permissible to inter-pret, and others attach it to the inner sense that it is not permissible for the learned to take according to its apparent sense. That is because this sort [of verses and Traditions] is recondite and abstruse. One who commits an error with respect to this is to be excused—I mean, one of the learned.

(32) If it were said, "Since it has become evident that, in this respect, there are three ranks in the Law, then in which of these three ranks, according to you, belongs what is set forth with respect to descriptions of the next life and its conditions?" we would say, "With respect to this question, it is an evident matter that they belong to the sort about which there is disagreement." That is because we see | a group who pretend to

(٣٠) ومن هذا الصنف آية الاستواء وحديث النزول. ولذلك قال عليه السلام في السوداء إذ أخبرته أن الله في السماء «اعتقها فإنها مؤمنة» إذ كانت ليست من أهل البرهان. والسبب في ذلك أن الصنف من الناس الذين لا يقع لهم التصديق إلا من قبل التخيل ٥ — أعني أنهم لا يصدقون بالشيء إلا من جهة ما يتخيلونه — يعسر وقوع التصديق لهم.بموجود ليس منسوبا إلى شيء متخيَّل.

ويدخل أيضا على من لا يفهم من هذه النسبة إلا المكان، وهم الذين بعدوا عن رتبة الصنف الأول قليلا في النظر اعتقاد الجسمية. ولذلك كان الجواب لهؤلاء في أمثال هذه أنها من المتشابهات وأن ١٠ الوقف في قوله تعالى ﴿وَمَا يَعْلَمُ تَأْوِيلَهُ إِلَّا ٱللهُ﴾ [٧:٣]. وأهل البرهان مع أنهم مجمعون في هذا الصنف أنه من المؤوَّل فقد يختلفون في تأويله، وذلك بحسب مرتبة كل واحد من معرفة البرهان.

(٣١) وههنا صنف ثالث من الشرع متردد بين هذين الصنفين يقع فيه شك، فيُلحقه قوم ممن يتعاطى النظر بالظاهر الذي لا يجوز تأويله ويُلحقه آخرون بالباطن الذي لا يجوز حمله على الظاهر ١٥ للعلماء، وذلك لعواصة هذا الصنف واشتباهه. والمخطىء في هذا معذور، أعني من العلماء.

(٣٢) فإن قيل: فإذا تبيّن أن الشرع في هذا على ثلاث مراتب، فمن أيّ هذه المراتب الثلاث هو عندكم ما جاء في صفات المعاد وأحواله. فنقول: إن هذه المسألة الأمر فيها بيّن أنها من الصنف ٢٠ المختلَف فيه، وذلك أنا نرى [١٧] قوما ممن ينسبون أنفسهم إلى

demonstration, saying that it is obligatory to take these descriptions in their apparent sense since there is no demonstration rendering that apparent sense preposterous; and this is the method of the Ash°arites. Yet another group, who also occupy themselves with demonstration, interpret these descriptions; and they disagree greatly among themselves in their interpretation. Among this sort are to be counted Abū Ḥāmid [al-Ghazālī] and many of the Sufis. And some combine both interpretations, as Abū Ḥāmid [al-Ghazālī] does in some of his books.

(33) It seems that the learned person who commits an error with respect to this question is to be excused and the one who hits the mark is to be thanked or rewarded—that is, if he acknowledges the existence [of the next life] and gives a manner of interpretation of it not leading to the disavowal of its existence. With respect to this [question], denying its existence is what is unbelief, because it is one of the roots of the Law and something to which assent comes about by the three methods shared by "the red and the black."

(34) For anyone not adept in science, it is obligatory to take them [the descriptions of the next life] in their apparent sense; for him, it is unbelief to interpret them because it leads to unbelief. That is why we are of the opinion that, for anyone among the people whose duty it is to have faith in the apparent sense, interpretation is unbelief because it leads to unbelief. Anyone adept in interpretation who divulges that to him calls him to unbelief; and the one who calls to unbelief is an unbeliever.

(35) This is why it is obligatory that interpretations be established only in books using demonstrations. For if they are in books using demonstrations, no one but those adept in demonstration will get at them. Whereas, if they are established in other than demonstrative books with poetical and rhetorical or dialectical methods used in them, as Abū Ḥāmid [al-Ghazālī] does, that is an error against the Law and against wisdom.

البرهان يقولون إن الواجب حملها على ظواهرها إذ كان ليس ههنا برهان يؤدي إلى استحالة الظاهر فيها، وهذه طريقة الأشعرية، وقوم آخرون أيضا ممن يتعاطى البرهان يتأولونها وهؤلاء يختلفون في تأويلها اختلافا كثيرا. وفي هذا الصنف هو أبو حامد معدود ٥ وكثير من المتصوفة. ومنهم من يجمع فيها التأويلين كما يفعل ذلك أبو حامد في بعض كتبه.

(٣٣) ويشبه أن يكون المخطئ في هذه المسألة من العلماء معذورا والمصيب مشكورا أو مأجورا، وذلك إذا اعترف بالموجود وتأول فيها نحوا من أنحاء التأويل لا يؤدي إلى نفي الوجود. وإنما كان ١٠ جحد الوجود في هذه كفرا، لأنه في أصل من أصول الشريعة وهو مما يقع التصديق به بالطرق الثلاث المشتركة «الأحمر والأسود».

(٣٤) وأما من كان من غير أهل العلم فالواجب عليه حملها على ظاهرها وتأويلها في حقه كفر لأنه يؤدي إلى الكفر. ولذلك ما نرى أن من كان من الناس فرضه الإيمان بالظاهر فالتأويل في ١٥ حقه كفر لأنه يؤدى إلى الكفر، فمن أفشاه له من أهل التأويل فقد دعاه إلى الكفر، والداعي إلى الكفر كافر.

(٣٥) ولهذا يجب أن لا تُثبَت التأويلات إلا في كتب البراهين، لأنها إذا كانت في كتب البراهين لم يصل إليها إلا من هو من أهل البرهان. فأما إذا أثبتت في غير كتب البرهان واستُعمل فيها الطرق ٢٠ الشعرية والخطابية أو الجدلية كما يصنعه أبو حامد، فخطأ على الشرع وعلى الحكمة.

Yet the man intended only good. That is, he wished thereby to make those adept in science more numerous. But he actually made those adept in wickedness more numerous, yet not without some increase among those adept in science. In that way, one group came to slander wisdom, another group to slander the Law, and another group to reconcile the two. It seems that this was one of the intentions of | his books.

An indication that he wished thereby to alert people's minds[40] is that he adhered to no single doctrine in his books. Rather, with the Ashʿarites he was an Ashʿarite, with the Sufis a Sufi, and with the philosophers a philosopher—so that he was, as it is said:

> One day a Yamanī, if I meet a man from Yaman,
> And if I meet a Maʿaddi, then I'm of Adnān.[41]

(36) What is obligatory for the imams of the Muslims is that they ban those of his books that contain science from all but those adept in science, just as it is obligatory upon them to ban demonstrative books from those not adept in them. Yet the harm befalling people from demonstrative books is lighter, because for the most part only those with superior innate dispositions take up demonstrative books. And this sort [of people] is misled only through a lack of practical virtue, reading in a disorderly manner, and turning to them without a teacher.

Still, totally forbidding demonstrative books bars from what the Law calls to, because it is a wrong to the best sort of people and to the best sort of existing things. For justice with respect to the best sort of existing things is for them to be cognized to their utmost degree by those prepared to be cognizant of them to their utmost degree, and these are the best sort of people. Indeed, the greater the worth of the existing thing, the greater is the injustice with respect to it—namely, ignorance of it. Therefore, He said (may He be exalted), "Associating [other gods with God] is surely a major wrong" [31:13].[42]

وإن كان الرجل إنما قصد خيرا، وذلك أنه رام أن يكثر أهل العلم بذلك ولكن كثر بذلك أهل الفساد ليس بدون كثرة أهل العلم، وتطرق بذلك قوم إلى ثلب الحكمة وقوم إلى ثلب الشريعة وقوم إلى الجمع بينهما. ويشبه أن يكون هذا أحد مقاصده[١٨] بكتبه.

٥   والدليل على أنه رام بذلك تنبيه الفطر أنه لم يلزم مذهبا من المذاهب في كتبه، بل هو مع الأشعرية أشعري ومع الصوفية صوفي ومع الفلاسفة فيلسوف، حتى أنه كما قيل:

يوما يَمانٍ إذا لاقَيتُ ذا يَمن   وإن لَقِيتُ مَعَدِّيّا فَعَدنانِ

(٣٦) والذي يجب على أئمة المسلمين أن ينهوا عن كتبه التي

١٠ تتضمن العلم إلا لمن كان من أهل العلم، كما يجب لهم أن ينهوا عن كتب البرهان من ليس أهلا لها، وإن كان الضرر الداخل على الناس من كتب البرهان أخف، لأنه لا يقف على كتب البرهان في الأكثر إلا أهل الفطر الفائقة، وإنما يؤتى هذا الصنف من عدم الفضيلة العملية والقراءة على غير ترتيب وأخذها من غير معلم.

١٥   ولكن منعها بالجملة صاد لما دعا إليه الشرع لأنه ظلم لأفضل أصناف الناس ولأفضل أصناف الموجودات، إذ كان العدل في أفضل أصناف الموجودات أن يعرفها على كنهها من كان معَدا لمعرفتها على كنهها وهم أفضل أصناف الناس، فإنه على عظم قدر الموجود يعظم الجور في حقه الذي هو الجهل به. ولذلك قال

٢٠   تعالى «إِنَّ ٱلشِّرْكَ لَظُلْمٌ عَظِيمٌ» [٣١:١٣].

[IV. Summary]

(37) So this is what we were of the opinion we should establish with respect to this type of reflection—I mean, the discussion between the Law and wisdom and the statutes for interpreting the Law. If it were not for this being so widespread among people and these questions we have mentioned being so widespread, we would not have deemed it permissible to write a single letter about it; nor would we have to excuse ourselves to those adept in interpretation for doing so, because these questions are such as to be mentioned in demonstrative books. God is the Guide to and the Successful Giver of what is correct!

[v. On what is intended by the Law and its methods]

[A. What is intended by the Law]

(38) You ought to know that what is intended by the Law is only to teach true science and true practice. True science is cognizance of God (may He be blessed and exalted) and of all the existing things as they are, especially the venerable ones among them; and cognizance of happiness in the hereafter and of misery in the hereafter. True practice is to follow the actions that promote happiness | and to avoid the actions that promote misery; and cognizance of these actions is what is called "practical science."

These [actions] are divided into two divisions. One is the apparent, bodily actions. The science of these is what is called "jurisprudence." The second division is actions of the soul—like gratitude, patience, and other moral habits that the Law calls to or bans. And the science of these is what is called "asceticism" and "the sciences of the hereafter."

Abū Ḥāmid [al-Ghazālī] directed himself to this in his book. Since people had turned away from this type and become immersed in the other type—even though this type is more involved with piety, which is the cause of happiness—he called his book *The Revival of the Sciences of Religion*.

But we have digressed from the path we were on, so let us come back.

(٣٧) فهذا ما رأينا أن نثبته في هذا الجنس من النظر، أعني التكلم بين الشريعة والحكمة وأحكام التأويل في الشريعة. ولولا شهرة ذلك عند الناس وشهرة هذه المسائل التي ذكرناها، لما استجزنا أن نكتب في ذلك حرفا ولا أن نعتذر في ذلك لأهل التأويل بعذر لأن شأن هذه المسائل أن تُذكَر في كتب البرهان. والله الهادي والموفق للصواب.

(٣٨) وينبغي أن تعلم أن مقصود الشرع إنما هو تعليم العلم الحق والعمل الحق. والعلم الحق هو معرفة الله تبارك وتعالى وسائر الموجودات على ما هي عليه وبخاصة الشريفة منها، ومعرفة السعادة [١٩] الأخراوية والشقاء الأخراوي. والعمل الحق هو امتثال الأفعال التي تفيد السعادة وتجنب الأفعال التي تفيد الشقاء، والمعرفة بهذه الأفعال هو الذي يسمى «العلم العملي».

وهذه تنقسم قسمين، أحدهما أفعال ظاهرة بدنية، والعلم بهذه هو الذي يسمى «الفقه»، والقسم الثاني أفعال نفسانية مثل الشكر والصبر وغير ذلك من الأخلاق التي دعا إليها الشرع أو نهى عنها، والعلم بهذه هو الذي يسمى «الزهد» و«علوم الآخرة».

وإلى هذا نحا أبو حامد في كتابه، ولما كان الناس قد أضربوا عن هذا الجنس وخاضوا في الجنس الثاني وكان هذا الجنس أملك بالتقوى التي هي سبب السعادة، سمى كتابه «إحياء علوم الدين».

وقد خرجنا عما كنا بسبيله فنرجع.

(39) We say: Since what is intended by the Law is teaching true science and true practice; and teaching is of two sorts—forming a concept and bringing about assent—as those adept in dialectical theology have explained; and there are three methods of bringing about assent for
5   people—demonstrative, dialectical, and rhetorical—and two methods of forming concepts, either by means of the thing itself or by means of a likeness of it; and not all people have natures such as to accept demonstrations or dialectical arguments, let alone demonstrative arguments, given the difficulty in teaching demonstrative arguments and the lengthy
10   time needed by someone adept at learning them; and since what is intended by the Law is, indeed, to teach everyone, therefore, it is obligatory that the Law comprise all the manners of the methods of bringing about assent and all the manners of the methods of forming a concept.

[B. The methods in the Law for assent and concept]

(40) Since some of the methods for bringing about assent—I mean,
15   assent taking place because of them—are common to most people, namely, the rhetorical and the dialectical, the rhetorical being more common than the dialectical; and some of them are particular to fewer people, namely, the demonstrative; and what is primarily intended by the Law is taking care of the greater number without neglecting to alert
20   the select [few], therefore, most of the methods declared in the Law are the methods shared | by the greater number with respect to concept or assent taking place.

(41) There are four sorts of these methods in the Law.

One, even though it is shared, is particular[43] in both respects—I
25   mean that, with respect to forming a concept and bringing about assent, it is certain, even though it is rhetorical or dialectical. These syllogisms are the ones whose premises happen to be certain, even though they are

(٣٩) فنقول: لما كان مقصود الشرع تعليم العلم الحق والعمل الحق، وكان التعليم صنفين تصورا وتصديقا كما بيّن ذلك أهل العلم بالكلام، وكانت طرق التصديق الموجودة للناس ثلاثا البرهانية والجدلية والخطابية، وطرق التصور اثنين إما الشيء نفسه

٥ وإما مثاله، وكان الناس كلهم ليس في طباعهم أن يقبلوا البراهين ولا الأقاويل الجدلية فضلا عن البرهانية – مع ما في تعليم الأقاويل البرهانية من العسر والحاجة في ذلك إلى طول الزمان لمن هو أهل لتعلمها – وكان الشرع إنما مقصوده تعليم الجميع، وجب أن يكون الشرع يشتمل على جميع أنحاء طرق التصديق وأنحاء

١٠ طرق التصور.

(٤٠) ولما كانت طرق التصديق منها ما هي عامة لأكثر الناس – أعني وقوع التصديق من قبلها – وهي الخطابية والجدلية، والخطابية أعم من الجدلية، ومنها ما هي خاصة لأقل الناس وهي البرهانية، وكان الشرع مقصوده الأول العناية بالأكثر من غير

١٥ إغفال لتنبيه الخواص، كانت أكثر الطرق المصرح بها في الشريعة هي الطرق المشتركة[٢٠] للأكثر في وقوع التصور والتصديق.

(٤١) وهذه الطرق هي في الشريعة على أربعة أصناف: أحدها أن تكون مع أنها مشتركة خاصة في الأمرين جميعا، أعني أن تكون في التصور والتصديق يقينية مع أنها خطابية أو

٢٠ جدلية. وهذه المقاييس هي المقاييس التي عرض لمقدماتها مع كونها

generally accepted or suppositional, and whose conclusions happen to be
matters taken in themselves rather than as likenesses. For this sort of
Law-based statements there is no interpretation, and the one who denies
or interprets it is an unbeliever.

5   The premises in the second sort are certain, even though they are
generally accepted or suppositional, and the conclusions are likenesses
of the matters intended to be brought forth. This [sort of Law-based
statements]—I mean, its conclusions—admits of interpretation.

The third is the reverse of this, namely, that the conclusions are the
10   very matters intended to be brought forth, while the premises are generally accepted or suppositional without happening to be certain. For this
[sort of Law-based statements]—I mean, its conclusions—interpretation is not admitted either, but its premises may admit of it.

The premises in the fourth are generally accepted or suppositional
15   without happening to be certain, and its conclusions are likenesses of the
matter intended to be brought forth. With respect to these [Law-based
statements], the duty of the select is to interpret them, and the duty of
the multitude is to let them stand in their apparent sense.

(42) In general, with respect to everything in these [Law-based
20   statements] admitting of an interpretation apprehended only by demonstration, the duty of the select is that interpretation, whereas the duty of
the multitude is to take them in their apparent sense in both respects—
I mean, with respect to concept and assent—for there is nothing more
than that in their natures.

25   (43) Interpretations may occur to those who reflect upon the Law
due to the superiority some of these shared methods have over others
with respect to bringing about assent—I mean, when the indication of
the interpretation is more completely persuasive than the indication of the
apparent sense. Interpretations such as these are for the multitude, and
30   it is possible that they become a duty for those whose reflective powers

مشهورة أو مظنونة أن تكون يقينية، وعرض لنتائجها أن أخذت أنفسها دون مثالاتها. وهذا الصنف من الأقاويل الشرعية ليس له تأويل، والجاحد له أو المؤول كافر.

والصنف الثاني أن تكون المقدمات مع كونها مشهورة أو مظنونة يقينية، وتكون النتائج مثالات للأمور التي قُصد إنتاجها. وهذا يتطرق إليه التأويل، أعني لنتائجه.

والثالث عكس هذا، وهو أن تكون النتائج هي الأمور التي قُصد إنتاجها نفسها، وتكون المقدمات مشهورة أو مظنونة من غير أن يعرض لها أن تكون يقينية. وهذا أيضا لا يتطرق إليه تأويل، أعني لنتائجه، وقد يتطرق لمقدماته.

والرابع أن تكون مقدماته مشهورة أو مظنونة من غير أن يعرض لها أن تكون يقينية، وتكون نتائجه مثالات لما قُصد إنتاجه. وهذه فرض الخواص فيها التأويل، وفرض الجمهور إمرارها على ظاهرها.

(٤٢) وبالجملة فكل ما يتطرق له من هذه تأويل لا يُدرَك إلا بالبرهان، ففرض الخواص فيه هو ذلك التأويل، وفرض الجمهور هو حملها على ظاهرها في الوجهين جميعا، أعني في التصور والتصديق، إذ كان ليس في طباعهم أكثر من ذلك.

(٤٣) وقد يعرض للنظار في الشريعة تأويلات من قبل تفاضل الطرق المشتركة بعضها على بعض في التصديق، أعني إذا كان دليل التأويل أتم إقناعا من دليل الظاهر. وأمثال هذه التأويلات هي جمهورية، ويمكن أن يكون فرض من بلغت قواهم النظرية إلى القوة

reach that of dialectic. Into this type enter | some of the interpretations of the Ashᶜarites and the Muᶜtazilites,[44] although for the most part the statements of the Muᶜtazilites are more reliable. The duty of those within the multitude who are not capable of more than rhetorical statements is to let them stand in their apparent sense, and it is not permissible for them to know that interpretation at all.

[C. The three sorts of people and the Law's provision for them]

(44) For people are of three sorts with respect to the Law.

One sort is in no way adept at interpretation. These are the rhetorical people, who are the overwhelming multitude. That is because no person of unimpaired intellect is exempted from this kind of assent.

Another sort is those adept in dialectical interpretation. These are those who are dialectical by nature alone, or by nature and by habit.

Another sort is those adept in certain interpretation. These are those who are demonstrative by nature and art—I mean, the art of wisdom. This interpretation ought not to be declared to those adept in dialectic, not to mention the multitude.

(45) When something pertaining to these interpretations is declared to someone not adept in them—especially demonstrative interpretations, due to their remoteness from things about which there is shared cognizance—both he who declares it and the one to whom it is declared are steered to unbelief. The reason is that interpretation includes two things: the rejection of the apparent sense and the establishing of the interpretation. Thus, if the apparent sense is rejected by someone who is an adept of the apparent sense without the interpretation being established for him, that leads him to unbelief if it is about the roots of the Law. So interpretations ought not to be declared to the multitude, nor established in rhetorical or dialectical books—I mean, books in

الجدلية. وفي هذا الجنس يدخل[٢١] بعض تأويلات الأشعرية والمعتزلة، وإن كانت المعتزلة في الأكثر أوثق أقوالا. وأما الجمهور الذين لا يقدرون على أكثر من الأقاويل الخطابية ففرضهم إمرارها على ظاهرها، ولا يجوز أن يعلموا ذلك التأويل أصلا.

(٤٤) فإذاً الناس في الشريعة على ثلاثة أصناف:

صنف ليس هو من أهل التأويل أصلا، وهم الخطابيون الذين هم الجمهور الغالب، وذلك أنه ليس يوجد أحد سليم العقل يعرى من هذا النوع من التصديق.

وصنف هو من أهل التأويل الجدلي، وهؤلاء هم الجدليون بالطبع فقط أو بالطبع والعادة.

وصنف هو من أهل التأويل اليقيني، وهؤلاء هم البرهانيون بالطبع والصناعة، أعني صناعة الحكمة. وهذا التأويل ليس ينبغي أن يصرّح به لأهل الجدل فضلا عن الجمهور.

(٤٥) ومتى صُرح بشيء من هذه التأويلات لمن هو من غير أهلها، وبخاصة التأويلات البرهانية لبعدها عن المعارف المشتركة، أفضى ذلك بالمصرّح به والمصرّح له إلى الكفر. والسبب في ذلك أن التأويل يتضمن شيئين إبطال الظاهر وإثبات المؤوَّل، فإذا بطل الظاهر عند من هو من أهل الظاهر ولم يثبت المؤوَّل عنده أداه ذلك إلى الكفر، إن كان في أصول الشريعة. فالتأويلات ليس ينبغي أن يصرّح بها للجمهور ولا أن تُثبَت في الكتب الخطابية أو الجدلية –

which the statements posited are of these two sorts—as Abū Ḥāmid [al-Ghazālī] did.[45]

(46) For this kind [of people], it is obligatory to declare and to say, with respect to the apparent sense—when it is such that the doubt as to whether it is an apparent sense is in itself apparent to everyone, without cognizance of its interpretation being possible for them—that it is one of those [verses] that resemble one another [whose interpretation is] not known, except to God, and that it is obligatory for the stop in His saying (may He be exalted) to be placed here: "None knows their interpretation but God" [3:7].[46] In the same way is the answer to come forth with respect to a question about obscure matters for whose understanding no path exists for the multitude—as with His saying (may He be exalted), "And they will ask you about the spirit; say: 'The spirit is by the command of my Lord; and of knowledge you have been given only a little'" [17:85].

(47) Now, | anyone who declares these interpretations to those not adept in them is an unbeliever because of his calling people to unbelief. This is contrary to the call of the Lawgiver, especially when they are corrupt interpretations having to do with the roots of the Law—as has occurred with a group of people in our time. For we have witnessed some groups who suppose they are philosophizing and have, by means of their astounding wisdom, apprehended things that disagree with the Law in every manner—I mean, [things] not admitting of interpretation. And [they suppose] that it is obligatory to declare these things to the multitude. By declaring those corrupt beliefs to the multitude, they have become the reason for the multitude's and their own perdition in this world and in the hereafter.

(48) Here is a likeness of these people's intention as contrasted to the intention of the Lawgiver: Someone is intent upon [going to] a skilled physician who is intent upon preserving the health of all of the people and removing sicknesses from them by setting down for them statements to which there is common assent[47] about the obligation of practicing the things that preserve their health and remove their sicknesses, as well as of avoiding the contrary things. He is not able to make them

أعني الكتب التي الأقاويل الموضوعة فيها من هذين الصنفين – كما صنع ذلك أبو حامد.

(٤٦) ولهذا الجنس يجب أن يصرَّح ويقال في الظاهر الذي الإشكال في كونه ظاهراً <ظاهر> للجميع بنفسه وكون معرفة تأويله غير ممكن فيهم – إنه متشابه لا يعلمه إلا الله، وإن الوقف يجب ههنا في قوله تعالى «وَمَا يَعْلَمُ تَأْوِيلَهُ إِلَّا آلله» [٣:٧]. وبمثل هذا يأتي الجواب أيضا في السؤال عن الأمور الغامضة التي لا سبيل للجمهور إلى فهمها، مثل قوله تعالى «وَيَسْأَلُونَكَ عَنِ ٱلرُّوحِ قُلِ ٱلرُّوحُ مِنْ أَمْرِ رَبِّى وَمَآ أُوتِيتُم مِّنَ ٱلْعِلْمِ إِلَّا قَلِيلاً» [٨٥:١٧].

(٤٧) وأما [٢٢] المصرَّح بهذه التأويلات لغير أهلها فكافر لمكان دعائه الناس إلى الكفر. وهو ضد دعوى الشارع، وبخاصة متى كانت تأويلات فاسدة في أصول الشريعة كما عرض ذلك لقوم من أهل زماننا. فإنا قد شاهدنا منهم أقواما ظنوا أنهم تفلسفوا وأنهم قد أدركوا بحكمتهم العجيبة أشياء مخالفة للشرع من جميع الوجوه، أعني لا تقبل تأويلا، وأن الواجب هو التصريح بهذه الأشياء للجمهور. فصاروا بتصريحهم للجمهور بتلك الاعتقادات الفاسدة سببا لهلاك الجمهور وهلاكهم في الدنيا والآخرة.

(٤٨) ومثال مقصد هؤلاء مع مقصد الشارع مثال من قصد إلى طبيب ماهر قصد إلى حفظ صحة جميع الناس وإزالة الأمراض عنهم بأن وضع لهم أقاويل مشتركة التصديق في وجوب استعمال الأشياء التي تحفظ صحتهم وتزيل أمراضهم وتجنَّب أضدادها، اذ لم

all become physicians, because the physician is the one who knows by demonstrative methods the things that preserve health and remove sickness. Then this one goes out to the people and says to them, "These methods this physician has set down for you are not true." And he sets about rejecting them until they have rejected them. Or he says, "They have interpretations." Yet they do not understand them and thus come to no assent as to what to do because of them.

Now are you of the opinion that people who are in this condition will do any of the things useful for preserving health and removing sickness? Or will this one who has declared that they should reject what they used to believe about those [things] be able to practice that with them— I mean, preserving health? No! Rather, he will not be able to practice these with them, nor will they be able to practice them; and perdition will encompass them all.

(49) This is if he declares sound interpretations about those things to them, because of their not understanding that interpretation—not to mention his declaring corrupt interpretations to them. Because he will so interpret the matter to them that they will not be of the opinion that there is a health that must be preserved or a sickness that must be removed, not to mention | their being of the opinion that there are things such as to preserve health and remove sickness. And this is what happens with respect to the Law when anyone declares an interpretation to the multitude or to someone not adept for it. He corrupts it and bars them from it; and the one who bars others from the Law is an unbeliever.

(50) Now this illustration is certain and not poetical, as someone might say. It is a sound linking between the one and the other. That is because the link between the physician and the health of bodies is [the same as] the link between the Lawgiver and the health of souls—I mean,

يمكنه أن يصير جميعهم أطباء لأن الذي يعلم الأشياء الحافظة للصحة والمزيلة للمرض بالطرق البرهانية هو الطبيب. فتهدي هذا إلى الناس وقال لهم إن هذه الطرق التي وضع لكم هذا الطبيب ليست بحق، وشرع في إبطالها حتى بطلت عندهم. أو قال إن لها تأويلات، فلم يفهموها ولا وقع لهم من قبلها تصديق في العمل. ٥

أفترى الناس الذين حالهم هذه الحال يفعلون شيئا من الأشياء النافعة في حفظ الصحة وإزالة المرض، أو يقدر هذا المصرح لهم بإبطال ما كانوا يعتقدون فيها أن يستعملها معهم، أعني حفظ الصحة. لا، بل ما يقدر هو لا على استعمالها معهم ولا هم يستعملونها، فيشملهم الهلاك. ١٠

(٤٩) هذا إن صرح لهم بتأويلات صحيحة في تلك الأشياء لكونهم لا يفهمون ذلك التأويل، فضلا أن صرح لهم بتأويلات فاسدة، لأنه يؤول بهم الأمر إلى أن لا يروا أن ههنا صحة يجب أن تُحفَظ ولا مرضا يجب أن يُزال، فضلا عن [٢٣] أن يروا أن ههنا أشياء تحفظ الصحة وتزيل المرض. وهذه هي حال من يصرح ١٥ بالتأويل للجمهور ولمن ليس هو بأهل له مع الشرع، ولذلك هو مفسد له وصاد عنه، والصاد عن الشرع كافر.

(٥٠) وإنما كان هذا التمثيل يقينيا وليس بشعري كما لقائل أن يقول، لأنه صحيح التناسب. وذلك إن نسبة الطبيب إلى صحة الأبدان نسبة الشارع إلى صحة الأنفس، أعني أن الطبيب هو الذي ٢٠

the physician is the one who seeks to preserve the health of bodies when it exists and to bring it back when it has disappeared, while the Lawgiver is the one who aspires to this with respect to the health of souls.

This health is what is called "piety." And the precious Book has declared in various verses that it is to be sought by means of Law-based actions. Thus, He (may He be exalted) said, "Fasting was prescribed for you, just as it was prescribed for those before you, so that you might come to be pious" [2:183]. And He (may He be exalted) said, "Neither their flesh nor their blood will reach God, but piety on your part will reach Him" [22:37].[48] And He said, "Indeed, prayer puts an end to iniquity and to transgression" [29:45]; and so on in innumerable other verses to this effect contained in the precious Book.

Now the Lawgiver seeks this health only through Law-based knowledge and Law-based practice. And this health is the one from which happiness in the hereafter derives and misery in the hereafter from its contrary.

(51) From this, it has become evident to you that sound interpretations—not to mention corrupt ones—must not be established in books for the multitude. Sound interpretation is the deposit mankind was charged with holding, and held, whereas all existing things shirked it— I mean the one mentioned in His statement (may He be exalted), "Indeed, we offered the deposit to the heavens, to the earth, and to the mountains," [and so on to the end of] the verse [33:72].[49]

[VI. On the emergence of factions within Islam]

[A. Different opinions regarding interpretation]

(52) Because of the interpretations with respect to the Law— especially the corrupt ones—and the supposition that it is obligatory to declare them to everyone, factions emerged within Islam so that one charged the others with unbelief or with heretical innovation. Thus, the

يطلب أن يحفظ صحة الأبدان إذا وُجدت ويستردها إذا ذهبت، والشارع هو الذي يبتغي هذا في صحة الأنفس.

وهذه الصحة هي المسماة بـ«التقوى». وقد صرح الكتاب العزيز بطلبها بالأفعال الشرعية في غير ما آية، فقال تعالى «كُتِبَ عَلَيْكُمُ ٱلصِّيَامُ كَمَا كُتِبَ عَلَى ٱلَّذِينَ مِن قَبْلِكُمْ لَعَلَّكُمْ تَتَّقُونَ» [٢:١٨٣]، وقال تعالى «لَن يَنَالَ ٱللَّه لُحُومُهَا وَلاَ دِمَآؤُهَا وَلَٰكِن يَنَالُهُ ٱلتَّقْوَىٰ مِنكُمْ» [٢٢:٣٧] وقال «إِنَّ ٱلصَّلَوٰةَ تَنْهَىٰ عَنِ ٱلْفَحْشَآءِ وَٱلْمُنكَرِ» [٢٩:٤٥]، إلى غير ذلك من الآيات التي تضمنها الكتاب العزيز من هذا المعنى.

فالشارع إنما يطلب بالعلم الشرعي والعمل الشرعي هذه الصحة، وهذه الصحة هي التي تترتب عليها السعادة الأخراوية، وعلى ضدها الشقاء الأخراوي.

(٥١) فقد تبيّن لك من هذا أنه ليس يجب أن تُثبَت التأويلات الصحيحة في الكتب الجمهورية فضلا عن الفاسدة. والتأويل الصحيح هي الأمانة التي حُملها الإنسان فحملها وأشفق منها جميع الموجودات، أعني المذكورة في قوله تعالى «إِنَّا عَرَضْنَا ٱلْأَمَانَةَ عَلَى ٱلسَّمَوَاتِ وَٱلْأَرْضِ وَٱلْجِبَالِ» الآية [٧٢:٣٣].

(٥٢) ومن قِبَل التأويلات والظن بأنها مما يجب أن يصرَّح بها في الشرع للجميع نشأت فرق الإسلام حتى كفر بعضهم بعضا وبدع بعضهم بعضا، وبخاصة الفاسدة منها. فتأولت المعتزلة

Mu᷄tazilites interpreted many verses and many Traditions and declared
their interpretations to the multitude, as did the Ash᷄arites, although
they resorted less to | interpretation. Because of that, they threw people
into loathing, mutual hatred, and wars; they tore the Law to shreds; and
5   they split the people up into every sort of faction.

(53) In addition to all this, in the methods they followed to establish
their interpretations they were neither with the multitude nor with the
select. They were not with the multitude because their methods were
more obscure than the methods shared by the majority. And they were
10   not with the select because, if their methods are examined, they are
found to fall short of the conditions for demonstration—and that will
be grasped after the slightest examination by anyone who is cognizant
of the conditions for demonstration. Rather, many of the roots upon
which the Ash᷄arites base their cognizance are sophistical. For they deny
15   many necessary things, such as the stability of accidents, the influence
of some things upon others, the existence of necessary reasons for what
is made to occur,[50] substantial forms, and intermediates.

(54) Those among them who reflect have wronged the Muslims in
the sense that a group of Ash᷄arites has charged with unbelief anyone
20   who is not cognizant of the existence of the Creator (glorious is He) by
the methods they have set down for cognizance of Him in their books.
But, in truth, they are the ones who are the unbelievers and those who
are misguided. From here on they disagreed, with one group saying,
"The first obligation is reflection," and another group saying, "Faith
25   is"—I mean, because they were not cognizant of which methods are
the ones shared by everyone through whose doors the Law calls all the
people and supposed that there is [only] one method. So they erred
about the intention of the Lawgiver and were misguided and made
others become misguided.

آيات كثيرة وأحاديث كثيرة وصرحوا بتأويلهم للجمهور، وكذلك
فعلت الأشعرية وإن كانت أقل [٢٤] تأويلا. فأوقعوا الناس من قِبَل
ذلك في شنآن وتباغض وحروب، ومزقوا الشرع وفرقوا الناس
كل التفريق.

(٥٣) وزائد إلى هذا كله طرقهم التي سلكوها في إثبات
تأويلاتهم ليسوا فيها لا مع الجمهور ولا مع الخواص – أما مع
الجمهور فلكونها <أ>غمض من الطرق المشتركة للأكثر، وأما مع
الخواص فلكونها إذا تؤُمِّلت وُجدت ناقصة عن شرائط البرهان،
وذلك يقف عليه بأدنى تأمل من عرف شرائط البرهان. بل كثير من
الأصول التي بنت عليها الأشعرية معارفها هي سوفسطائية، فإنها
تجحد كثيرا من الضروريات مثل ثبوت الأعراض وتأثير الأشياء
بعضها في بعض ووجود الأسباب الضرورية للمسبَّبات والصور
الجوهرية والوسائط.

(٥٤) ولقد تعدى نظارهم في هذا المعنى على المسلمين، أن
فرقة من الأشعرية كفرت من ليس يعرف وجود الباري سبحانه
بالطرق التي وضعوها لمعرفته في كتبهم، وهم الكافرون الضالون
بالحقيقة. ومن هنا اختلفوا فقال قوم ((أول الواجبات النظر)) وقال
قوم ((الإيمان))، أعني من قبل أنهم لم يعرفوا أي الطرق هي الطرق
المشتركة للجميع التي دعا الشرع من أبوابها جميع الناس، وظنوا
أن ذلك طريق واحد، فأخطأوا مقصد الشارع وضلوا وأضلوا.

[B. How to avoid the evils brought about by factions]

(55) If it were said, "If these methods followed by the Ashᶜarites and others adept in reflection are not the shared methods by which the Law-giver intended to teach the multitude and by which alone it is possible to teach them, then which ones are these methods in this Law of ours?" we would say: "They are the methods that are established in the precious Book alone. For if the precious Book is examined, the three methods existing for all the people will be found in it; and these are the shared methods for teaching the majority of the people and [the method for teaching] the select.[51] And if the matter is examined with respect to them, it will become apparent that no better shared methods for teaching the multitude are to be encountered than the methods mentioned in it."

(56) So anyone who distorts these methods by making an interpretation that is not apparent in itself or that is more apparent to everyone than they are—and that is something nonexistent—rejects | their wisdom and rejects their intended action for procuring human happiness. That is very apparent from the condition of those in the earliest days [of Islam] and the condition of those who came after them. For those in the earliest days came to have perfect virtue and piety only by practicing these statements, without making interpretations of them; and any one of them who grasped an interpretation did not think fit to declare it. When those who came after them practiced interpretation, their piety decreased, their disagreements became more numerous, their love for one another was removed, and they split up into factions.

(57) It is obligatory for whoever wants to remove this heretical inno-vation from the Law to apply himself to the precious Book and pick from it the indications existing for every single thing we are responsible for believing. In his reflection he is to strive for their apparent sense as much as he can without interpreting anything, except insofar as the interpretation is apparent in itself—I mean, of an apparentness shared by everyone. For if the statements set down in the Law for teaching the

(٥٥) فإن قيل: فإذا لم تكن هذه الطرق التي سلكتها الأشعرية وغيرهم من أهل النظر هي الطرق المشتركة التي قصد الشارع تعليم الجمهور بها التي لا يمكن تعليمهم بغيرها، فأيّ الطرق هي هذه الطرق في شريعتنا هذه. قلنا: هي الطرق التي ثبتت في الكتاب العزيز فقط، فإن الكتاب العزيز إذا تُؤمِّل وُجدت فيه الطرق الثلاث الموجودة لجميع الناس، و ‹هذه هي› الطرق المشتركة لتعليم أكثر الناس والخاصة. وإذا تُؤمِّل الأمر فيها ظهر أنه ليس يُلفى طرق مشتركة لتعليم الجمهور أفضل من الطرق المذكورة فيه.

(٥٦) فمن حرفها بتأويل لا يكون ظاهرا بنفسه، أو أظهر منها للجميع – وذلك شيء غير موجود – فقد أبطل [٢٥] حكمتها وأبطل فعلها المقصود في إفادة السعادة الإنسانية. وذلك ظاهر جدا من حال الصدر الأول وحال من أتى بعدهم، فإن الصدر الأول إنما صار إلى الفضيلة الكاملة والتقوى باستعمال هذه الأقاويل دون تأويلات فيها، ومن كان منهم وقف على تأويل لم ير أن يصرح به. وأما من أتى بعدهم فإنهم لما استعملوا التأويل قلَّ تقواهم وكثر اختلافهم وارتفعت محبتهم وتفرقوا فرقا.

(٥٧) فيجب على من أراد أن يرفع هذه البدعة عن الشريعة أن يعمد إلى الكتاب العزيز فيلتقط منه الاستدلالات الموجودة في شيء شيء مما كلفنا اعتقاده، ويجتهد في نظره ظاهرها ما أمكنه من غير أن يتأول من ذلك شيئا، إلا إذا كان التأويل ظاهرا بنفسه – أعني ظهورا مشتركا للجميع. فإن الأقاويل الموضوعة في الشرع لتعليم

people are examined, it seems that one reaches a point in defending them such that only someone who is an adept at demonstration pulls out of their apparent sense something that is not apparent in them. And this particular characteristic is not found in any other statements.

5   (58) The statements of the Law declared to everyone in the precious Book have three particular characteristics that indicate their inimitability. The first is that nothing more completely persuasive and able to bring about assent for everyone is to be found than they. The second is that by their nature they admit of defense, ending up at a point where
10   no one grasps an interpretation of them—if they are such as to have an interpretation—except those adept in demonstration. The third is that they contain a means of alerting those adept in the truth to the true interpretation. And this is not found in the doctrines of the Ashᶜarites, nor in the doctrines of the Muᶜtazilites—I mean, their interpretation
15   neither admits of defense, nor contains a means of alerting to the truth, nor is true. Therefore, innovative heresies have increased.

[VII. Conclusion]

[A. The need to pursue the task set forth here]

(59) We would love to devote ourselves to this intention and carry it out thoroughly; and if God prolongs our life, we shall establish as much of it as we can. That could possibly be a starting point for someone who
20   comes afterwards. Now our soul is in | utmost sorrow and pain due to the corrupt dissensions and distorted beliefs that have permeated this Law, especially those that have occurred to it from among people linking themselves to wisdom. For injuries from a friend are graver than injuries from an enemy—I mean that wisdom is the companion of the Law and its
25   milk sister. So injuries from those linked to it are the gravest injuries— apart from the enmity, hatred, and quarreling they bring about between both of them. These two are companions by nature and lovers by essence

الناس إذا تُؤمِّلت، يشبه أن يبلغ من نصرتها إلى حد لا يُخرج عن ظاهرها ما هو منها ليس على ظاهره إلا من كان من أهل البرهان. وهذه الخاصة ليس توجد لغيرها من الأقاويل.

(٥٨) فإن الأقاويل الشرعية المصرَّح بها في الكتاب العزيز للجميع لها ثلاث خواص دلت علي الإعجاز: إحداها أنه لا يوجد أتم إقناعا وتصديقا للجميع منها، والثانية أنها تقبل النصرة بطبعها إلى أن تنتهي إلى حد لا يقف على التأويل فيها – إن كانت مما فيها تأويل – إلا أهل البرهان، والثالثة أنها تتضمن التنبيه لأهل الحق على التأويل الحق. وهذا ليس يوجد لا في مذاهب الأشعرية ولا في مذاهب المعتزلة، أعني أن تأويلهم لا يقبل النصرة ولا يتضمن التنبيه على الحق ولا هو حق. ولذلك كثرت البدع.

(٥٩) وبودنا لو تفرغنا لهذا المقصد وقدرنا عليه، وإن أنسأ الله في العمر فسنثبت فيه قدر ما تيسر لنا منه، فعسى أن يكون ذلك مبدأ لمن يأتي بعد. فإن النفس مما تخلل [٢٦] هذه الشريعة من الأهواء الفاسدة والاعتقادات المحرَّفة في غاية الحزن والتألم، وبخاصة ما عرض لها من ذلك من قبل من ينسب نفسه إلى الحكمة. فإن الأذاية من الصديق هي أشد من الأذاية من العدو، أعني أن الحكمة هي صاحبة الشريعة والأخت الرضيعة، فالأذاية ممن يُنسَب إليها هي أشد الأذاية – مع ما توقع بينهما من العداوة والبغضاء والمشاجرة وهما المصطحبتان بالطبع المتحابتان بالجوهر

and instinct. It [the Law] has also been injured by many ignorant friends
from among those who link themselves to it, namely, the factions existing
within it. But God shows all people the right way, brings everyone to love
Him, unites their hearts in pious fear of Him, and removes hatred and
5   loathing from them through His grace and mercy.

[B. The positive role of the present rulership]

(60) God has removed many of these evils, ignorant occurrences,
and misguided paths by means of this triumphant rule.[52] By means of it,
He has brought many good things closer, especially for that sort who follow the path of reflection and yearn for cognizance of the truth. That is,
10   this rule calls the multitude to a middle method for being cognizant of
God (glorious is He), raised above the low level of the traditionalists yet
below the turbulence of the dialectical theologians, and alerts the select
to the obligation for complete reflection on the root of the Law. By His
grace, God is the Giver of success and the Guide.

والغريزة. وقد آذاها أيضا كثير من الأصدقاء الجهال ممن ينسبون أنفسهم إليها، وهي الفرق الموجودة فيها. والله يسدد الكل ويوفق الجميع لمحبته ويجمع قلوبهم على تقواه ويرفع عنهم البغض والشنآن بفضله ورحمته.

٥ (٦٠) وقد رفع الله كثيرا من هذه الشرور والجهالات والمسالك المضلات بهذا الأمر الغالب، وطرق به إلى كثير من الخيرات، وبخاصة على الصنف الذين سلكوا مسلك النظر ورغبوا في معرفة الحق. وذلك أنه دعا الجمهور من معرفة الله سبحانه إلى طريق وسط ارتفع عن حضيض المقلدين وانحط عن تشغيب المتكلمين، ونبه ١٠ الخواص على وجوب النظر التام في أصل الشريعة. والله الموفق والهادي بفضله.

EPISTLE DEDICATORY

◆

The question mentioned by the
Shaykh Abū al-Walīd in the Decisive Treatise.

[I. Introduction]

(1) | May God prolong your might, continue to bless you, and hide you from the sources of calamities!

(2) Since, through your excellent discernment and noble nature, you have greatly surpassed those who engage in these sciences, and your pertinent reflection has culminated in your having grasped the doubt occurring with respect to the knowledge of the Eternal[1] (may He be glorified), due to its being connected to things generated from it, it is obligatory upon us, for the sake of truth and for the sake of putting an end to your perplexity, to resolve this doubt—after speaking about its determination. For one who is not cognizant of how to tie will not be able to loosen.

[II. Statement of the doubt]

(3) The doubt is inevitably like this: If all of these [things] are in God's knowledge (may He be glorified) before they come about, are they in His knowledge the same before their coming about, or are they in His knowledge at the moment of their existence other than the way they are in His knowledge before they exist? If we say that they are in God's knowledge at the moment of their existence other than the way they are in His knowledge before they exist, it results that eternal knowledge changes and that when they emerge from nonexistence[2] to existence additional knowledge is generated. That is preposterous for eternal knowledge. And, if we say that knowledge of them is one in both cases,

[١٢٨] المسألة التي ذكرها الشيخ أبو الوليد في «فصل المقال»

(١) أدام الله عزتكم وأبقى بركتكم وحجب عيون النوائب عنكم.

(٢) لما فقتم بجودة ذهنكم وكريم طبعكم كثيرا ممن يتعاطى هذه العلوم، وانتهى نظركم السديد إلى أن وقفتم على الشك العارض في علم القديم سبحانه مع كونه متعلقا بالأشياء المحدَثة عنه، وجب علينا لمكان الحق ولمكان إزالة هذه الشبهة عنكم أن نحل هذا الشك بعد أن نقول في تقريره. فإنه من لم يعرف الربط لم يقدر على الحل.

(٣) والشك يلزم هكذا: إن كانت هذه كلها في علم الله سبحانه قبل أن تكون، فهل هي في علمه كما كانت فيه قبل كونها، أم هي في علمه في حال وجودها على غير ما كانت عليه في علمه قبل أن توجد. فإن قلنا إنها في علم الله في حال وجودها على غير ما كانت عليه في علمه قبل أن توجد، لزم أن يكون العلم القديم متغيرا وأن يكون إذا خرجت من العدم إلى الوجود قد حدث هنالك علم زائد، وذلك مستحيل على العلم القديم. وإن قلنا إن العلم بها

it will be said, "Are they in themselves—that is, the generated beings—
before they exist as they are when they exist?" So it will be obligatory to
say, "They are not in themselves before they exist as they are when they
exist." Otherwise, existence and nonexistence would be one.

5   If the adversary admits this, it is to be said to him, "Is not true knowl-
edge cognizance of existence as it is?" If he says, "Yes," it is to be said, |
"From this it is obligatory that, when something differs in itself, knowledge of it differs; otherwise, it would be known in a way other than as it
is." Therefore, one of two matters is obligatory: either eternal knowledge
10   differs in itself, or generated things are not known to it. Both matters
are preposterous for it (may He be glorified).

         (4) What appears from the case of man confirms this doubt, I mean,
from his knowledge of nonexistent things being connected with the
assumption of existence and his knowledge of them being connected
15   [with it] when they exist. For it is self-evident that the two kinds of
knowledge differ from one another. Otherwise, he would be ignorant
of their existence at the moment in which they exist.

         (5) There is no escape from this through what the dialectical theolo-
gians have been accustomed to answer—namely, that He (may He be
20   exalted) knows things before they come to be as they will come to be at
the instant of their coming to be with respect to time, place, and the
other attributes particularly characteristic of each being. For it is said to
them, "When they exist, is a change then generated or not generated,
namely, in the emergence of the thing from nonexistence to existence?"
25   Now if they say, "It is not generated," they are being contentious. And,
if they say, "A change is then generated," it is to be said to them, "Is the
generation of this change known to eternal knowledge or not?" And the

واحد في الحالتين، قيل فهل هي في نفسها — أعني الموجودات
الحادثة — قبل أن توجد كما هي حين ما وجدت. فسيجب أن يقال
ليست في نفسها قبل أن توجد كما هي حين وجدت، وإلا كان
الموجود والمعدوم واحدا.

فإذا سلم الخصم هذا، قيل له أفليس العلم الحقيقي هو معرفة ٥
الوجود على ما هو عليه. فإذا قال نعم قيل[١٢٩] فيجب على هذا
إذا اختلف الشيء في نفسه أن يكون العلم به يختلف، وإلا فقد
عُلم على غير ما هو عليه. فإذاً يجب أحد أمرين، إما أن يختلف
العلم القديم في نفسه أو تكون الحادثات غير معلومة له، وكلا
الأمرين مستحيل عليه سبحانه. ١٠

(٤) ويؤكد هذا الشك ما يظهر من حال الإنسان، أعني من
تعلق علمه بالأشياء المعدومة على تقدير الوجود وتعلق علمه بها إذا
وجدت، فإنه من البين بنفسه أن العلمين متغايرين، وإلا كان جاهلا
بوجودها في الوقت الذي وجدت فيه.

(٥) وليس ينجي من هذا ما جرت به عادة المتكلمين في ١٥
الجواب عن هذا بأنه تعالى يعلم الأشياء قبل كونها على ما تكون
عليه في حين كونها من زمان ومكان وغير ذلك من الصفات
المختصة بموجود موجود. فإنه يقال لهم فإذا وجدت فهل حدث
هنالك تغير أو لم يحدث، وهو خروج الشيء من العدم إلى
الوجود. فإن قالوا لم يحدث فقد كابروا. وإن قالوا حدث هنالك ٢٠
تغير، قيل لهم فهل حدوث هذا التغير معلوم للعلم القديم أم لا،

previous doubt results. In sum, it is difficult to conceive that knowledge
of something before it exists and knowledge of it after it exists is the very
same knowledge.

So this is the determination of this doubt in the most profound way it
5   can be determined, as we have [previously] conversed with you about it.

[III. The solution]

(6) The solution of this doubt requires a long discussion. Here, however, we are intent upon [stating] the point by which it is to be resolved.
Abū Ḥāmid [al-Ghazālī] wanted to resolve this doubt in his book entitled *The Incoherence [of the Philosophers]* by means of something not per-
10   suasive. That is because he made a statement whose meaning is this: He
claimed that knowledge and what is known are related; and just as one
of two related things may change and the other related thing not change
in itself, so is it likely to occur with things in God's knowledge (may He
be glorified). That is, they change in themselves, but His knowledge of
15   them (may He be glorified) does not change.[3]

An example | of that with respect to what is related is for there to be
a single column on Zayd's right, then for it to come to be on his left while
Zayd would not have changed in himself. And that is not sound, for the
relation has changed in itself. That is, the relation that was right[-
20   handed] has come to be left[-handed]. What alone has not changed is
the subject of the relation, that is, the one bearing it—namely, Zayd. If
that is so and if knowledge is itself the relation, then it must have
changed when what is known changed, just as the relation of the column
to Zayd changes when it [the column] changes—that is, when it comes
25   to be left[-handed] after having been right[-handed].

(7) What resolves this doubt for us is to become cognizant that the
case for eternal knowledge with respect to existence is different from
the case for generated knowledge with respect to existence. That is

فيلزم الشك المتقدم. وبالجملة فيعسر أن يُتصوَّر أن العلم بالشيء قبل أن يوجد والعلم به بعد أن وجد علم واحد بعينه.

فهذا هو تقرير هذا الشك على أبلغ ما يمكن أن يُقرَّر به، على ما فاوضناكم فيه.

(٦) وحل هذا الشك يستدعي كلاما طويلا، إلا أنا ههنا نقصد ٥ للنكتة التي بها ينحل. وقد رام أبو حامد حل هذا الشك في كتابه الموسوم بـ«التهافت» بشيء ليس فيه مَقنَع، وذلك أنه قال قولا معناه هذا: وهو أنه زعم أن العلم والمعلوم من المضاف، وكما أنه قد يتغير أحد المضافين ولا يتغير المضاف الآخر في نفسه، كذلك يشبه أن يعرض للأشياء في علم الله سبحانه، أعني أن تتغير في ١٠ أنفسها ولا يتغير علمه سبحانه بها.

ومثال [١٣٠] ذلك في المضاف أنه قد تكون الأسطوانة الواحدة يمنة زيد ثم تعود يسرته وزيد بعد لم يتغير في نفسه. وليس بصادق، فإن الإضافة قد تغيرت في نفسها، وذلك أن الإضافة التي كانت يمنة قد عادت يسرة، وإنما الذي لم يتغير هو موضوع الإضافة، أعني الحامل لها ١٥ الذي هو زيد. وإذا كان ذلك كذلك وكان العلم هو نفس الإضافة، فقد يجب أن يتغير عند تغير المعلوم، كما تتغير إضافة الاسطوانة إلى زيد عند تغيرها، وذلك إذا عادت يسرة بعد أن كانت يمنة.

(٧) والذي ينحل له هذا الشك عندنا هو أن يُعرَف أن الحال في العلم القديم مع الموجود خلاف الحال في العلم المحدَث مع ٢٠

because existence is the cause and reason of our knowledge, while eternal knowledge is the cause and reason of existence. If additional knowledge comes to be generated in eternal knowledge when existence exists after having not existed, as that is generated in generated knowledge, it results

5   that eternal knowledge would be caused by existence—not be a cause for it. Thus, in that instance there must be no change generated such as is generated with respect to generated knowledge.

This error came forth only due to an analogy between eternal knowledge and generated knowledge—namely, an analogy between what is

10   not seen[4] and what is witnessed. And the wrongness of this analogy is recognized.[5] Just as no change is generated in the agent when what it brings about comes to exist—I mean, a change that was not there before—so no change is generated in eternal knowledge (may He be glorified) when what is known through it is generated.

[IV. Consequences]

15   (8) The doubt has therefore been resolved, nor is it inevitable for us that when no change is generated there—that is, in eternal knowledge— He does not know an existing being at the instant of its being generated as it really is. It results only that He knows it, not by means of generated knowledge, but by means of eternal knowledge, because change generated

20   in knowledge when there is change in existence is a stipulation only with respect to knowledge caused by existence—namely, generated knowledge.

(9) Therefore, eternal knowledge is connected with existence as | an attribute other than the one by which generated knowledge is connected with it. It is not that it is not at all connected, as it was related that the

25   philosophers said concerning this doubt, namely, that He (may He be glorified) does not know particulars. The matter is not as was fancied with respect to them. Rather, they are of the opinion that He does not know particulars by means of generated knowledge—a stipulation of which is that it is generated as they are generated—since He is a cause

الموجود، وذلك أن الموجود هو علة وسبب لعلمنا والعلم القديم هو
علة وسبب للموجود. فلو كان إذا وجد الموجود بعد أن لم يوجد
حدث في العلم القديم علم زائد كما يحدث ذلك في العلم المحدَث،
لزم أن يكون العلم القديم معلولا للموجود لا علة له. فإذاً واجب
أن لا يحدث هنالك تغير كما يحدث في العلم المحدث. ٥

وإنما أتى هذا الغلط من قياس العلم القديم على العلم المحدَث،
وهو قياس الغائب على الشاهد، وقد عُرف فساد هذا القياس.
وكما أنه لا يحدث في الفاعل تغير عند وجود مفعوله، أعني تغيرا
لم يكن قبل ذلك، كذلك لا يحدث في العلم القديم سبحانه تغير
عند حدوث معلومه عنه. ١٠

(٨) فإذاً قد انحل الشك، ولم يلزمنا أنه إذا لم يحدث هنالك
تغير، أعني في العلم القديم، فليس يعلم الموجود في حين حدوثه
على ما هو عليه، وإنما لزم ألا يعلمه بعلم محدَث إلا بعلم قديم، لأن
حدوث التغير في العلم عند تغير الموجود إنما هو شرط في العلم
المعلول عن الموجود، وهو العلم المحدث. ١٥

(٩) فإذاً العلم القديم إنما يتعلق بالموجود على[١٣١] صفة غير
الصفة التي يتعلق بها العلم المحدَث، لا أنه غير متعلق أصلا كما
حُكي عن الفلاسفة أنهم يقولون لموضع هذا الشك إنه سبحانه لا
يعلم الجزئيات. وليس الأمر كما تُوُهِّم عليهم، بل يرون أنه لا يعلم
الجزئيات بالعلم المحدَث الذي من شرطه الحدوث بحدوثها، إذ كان ٢٠

of them and not caused by them, as is the case with generated knowledge. This is the ultimate in removing imperfections [from God] that it
is obligatory to acknowledge.

[v. Conclusion]

(10) Now demonstration necessitates that He know things because
their originating from Him is only due to His knowing, not due to His
simply existing or existing with a particular attribute, but due to His
knowing—as He said (may He be exalted), "Does He not know, He who
created, the perspicacious, the experienced?" [67:14]. And demonstration requires that He not know them by means of knowledge that has
the attribute of generated knowledge. So for existing beings there must
be another knowledge, one that is not qualified. It is eternal knowledge
(may He be glorified). How can it be conceived that the Peripatetics
among the sages are of the opinion that eternal knowledge does not
include particulars, when they are of the opinion that it is the reason for
premonition with respect to dreams, revelation, and inspiration?[6]

(11) This is what appeared to us as a way of resolving this doubt. It is
a matter to be neither disputed nor doubted. God is the one who conduces to what is correct and guides to the truth. Peace be upon you, along
with God's mercy and His blessings!

علة لها لا معلولا عنها كالحال في العلم المحدَث. وهذا هو غاية التنزيه الذي يجب أن يُعترَف به.

(١٠) فإنه قد اضطر البرهان إلى أنه عالم بالأشياء لأن صدورها عنه إنما هو من جهة أنه عالم، لا من جهة أنه موجود فقط أو موجود بصفة كذا بل من جهة أنه عالم، كما قال تعالى ﴿ألا يَعْلَمُ مَنْ خَلَقَ وَهُوَ ٱللَّطِيفُ ٱلْخَبِيرُ﴾ [١٤:٦٧]. وقد اضطر البرهان إلى أنه غير عالم بها بعلم هو على صفة العلم المحدَث. فواجب أن يكون هنالك للموجودات علم آخر لا يُكيَّف، وهو العلم القديم سبحانه. وكيف يمكن أن يُتصوَّر أن المشائين من الحكماء يرون أن العلم القديم لا يحيط بالجزئيات، وهم يرون أنه سبب الإنذار في المنامات والوحي والإلهامات.

(١١) فهذا ما ظهر لنا في وجه حل هذا الشك، وهو أمر لا مرية فيه ولا شك. والله الموفق للصواب والمرشد للحق. والسلام عليكم ورحمة الله وبركاته.

Appendix

Averroës' defense of the philosophers as believing
in happiness and misery in the hereafter[1]

[I. Introduction]

(1) When he [al-Ghazālī] finished with these questions, he began to claim that the philosophers deny the resurrection of bodies. This is something for which no statement is found among any one of those who have gone before, although a statement about the resurrection of bodies has been widespread in Laws for at least a thousand years. Yet those from whom philosophy has come to us do not go back that many years. That is because the first to speak about the resurrection of bodies were the prophets of the children of Israel who came after Moses (peace upon him), and that is evident from the Psalms and from many of the writings attributed to the children of Israel. It is also established in the New Testament, and the statement has a tradition going back to Jesus (peace upon him). It is [also] a statement of the Sabaeans, and Abū Muḥammad ibn Ḥazm [581] says that theirs is the oldest of the Laws.

[II. The philosophers' opinions about Laws]

(2) But it appears that the group [of philosophers] is the people who make the most of them and have the most faith in them.[2] The reason for that is their being of the opinion that they [the Laws] direct to the governance of people by means of which a human being exists insofar as he is human and obtains the happiness particularly characteristic of one [a human being]. That is because they [the Laws] are necessary for the existence of the human moral virtues, theoretical virtues, and practical arts. And that is because they [the philosophers] are of the opinion that a human being has no life in this abode but by means of the practical arts, and no life in this abode or in the final abode but by means of the theoretical virtues; that neither one of these two is completed or obtained for him but by means of the moral virtues; and that the moral virtues are not firmly established but through cognizance of God (may He be exalted) and magnifying Him by means of the devotions set down in the

Law for them in each and every religion—such as offerings, prayers, invocations, and similar speeches spoken in praise of God (may He be exalted), the angels, and the prophets. In sum, they [the philosophers] are of the opinion that the Laws are the necessary civic arts whose principles are taken from the intellect and Legislation, especially those that are common to all the Laws—even if they [the Laws] do differ about the lesser and the greater with respect to that.

(3) They [the philosophers] are of the opinion, moreover, that one ought not to object to their common principles by means of a statement that establishes or rejects—such as whether it is obligatory to worship God [582] or not and, more than that, whether He exists or not. And they are of the same opinion with respect to the rest of the principles, such as the statement about the existence of final happiness and what it is like, because all Laws agree about another existence after death, even if they[3] differ about the description of that existence—just as they agree about His existence, attributes, and actions being cognizable, even if they differ in the lesser and the greater with respect to what they say about the essence of the Principle and His actions. Similarly, they agree about the actions that lead to the happiness of the final abode, even if they differ in the evaluation of these actions.

(4) In sum, since they [the Laws] had directed to wisdom by means of a path shared by all, they [the philosophers] held them [the Laws] to be obligatory. For philosophy directs to making only a few intelligent people cognizant of happiness, and it is up to them to learn wisdom, whereas the Laws are intent upon teaching the multitude in general. In spite of that, we do not find any one of the Laws that has not been attentive to what particularly characterizes the wise, even though it is concerned with what the multitude share in.

(5) Since the select sort of people completes its existence and attains its happiness only through association with the common sort, common education is necessary for the existence of the select sort and for its life both in the moment of its youth and its growing up—and no one doubts that—and as it passes on [583] to what particularly characterizes it. A necessity of the virtue of such a one[4] is not to make light of what he has grown up with; to interpret it in the fairest way; and to know that the intent of that education is what is common, not what is particular. And if he explicitly declares a doubt about the Law-based principles in which he has grown up or an interpretation contradicting the prophets (God's prayers upon them) and turning away from their path, then he is the person who most deserves to have the name of unbelief applied to him and to be judged with the penalty of unbelief in the religion in which he has grown up.

(6) In addition, it is obligatory upon him to choose the most virtuous one[5] in his time—even when all of them are true, according to him. He is to believe that the most virtuous will be abrogated by one more virtuous. Therefore, the wise men who were teaching the people of Alexandria became Muslim when the Law of Islam reached them. And the wise men who were in the cities of Byzantium became Christian when the Law of Jesus (peace upon him) reached them. And no one doubts that among the children of Israel there were many wise men. This is apparent from the books that are found among the

children of Israel attributed to Solomon (peace upon him). Nor has wisdom ever ceased to exist among those with revelation—namely, the prophets (peace upon them). Therefore, the truest of all propositions is that every prophet is a wise man, but not every wise man a prophet. Rather, they are the learned [584] of whom it is said that they are the heirs of the prophets.

(7) If the principles of the demonstrative arts are postulates and fundamentals that are posited, how much more appropriate must that be with respect to the Laws taken from revelation and intellect. Every Law comes about from revelation and has intellect mixed with it. For anyone who holds that it is possible for a Law to come about from intellect alone, it necessarily follows that it is more deficient than the Laws inferred from intellect and revelation. And everyone agrees that the principles of practice must be taken on authority, for there is no way to demonstrate what practice demands[6] except through the existence of virtues acquired through practical moral actions.

[iii. The superiority of the religion of Islam]

(8) Now it has become evident from this statement that wise men in their entirety are of this opinion with respect to the Laws—I mean, that the principles of action and the Traditions posited in each religion are to be taken on authority from the prophets. According to them, what is praiseworthy among these necessary principles is what most incites the multitude to virtuous actions, so that those brought up on these are more completely virtuous than those brought up on others—like it is with prayers among us. For there is no doubt that "prayer puts an end to iniquity and transgression," as God (may He be exalted) has said [29:45],[7] and that in the prayer posited in this Law this action is to be found more completely than in the rest of the prayers posited in the rest of the Laws, that is, with respect to what is stipulated as to their number, their times, their calling to mind, and the rest of what is stipulated with respect to them concerning purification and renouncing—I mean, renouncing actions and statements that corrupt them.

(9) The matter is the same with respect to the hereafter, for what is said in it urges more to virtuous actions that what is said in the others. Therefore, making an image of the hereafter for them [the people of the religion] by corporeal things is better than making an image of it by spiritual things, as He (may He be glorified) said, "The likeness of Paradise promised to the pious, from beneath which rivers flow" [13:35].[8] And the Prophet (peace upon him) said: "What is in it, no eye has seen, nor has ear heard, nor has it occurred to the mind of man." And Ibn ʿAbbās said, "There is nothing of this world in the world to come but names." He signified that that existence is another growth higher than this existence and another phase better than this phase. That is not to be denied by anyone who believes that we perceive a single existing thing being transformed from one phase to another, like inorganic forms being transformed until they come to perceive their [own] essences—namely, the intelligible forms. Those who doubt these things, object to that, and give expression to it are surely those intent upon rejecting the Laws and rejecting the virtues. They are the atheists who are of the opinion that a human being

has no end other than the enjoyment of pleasures—this no one doubts. Any of these who is capable of this will undoubtedly be killed by the companions of the Laws and by the wise in their entirety. For the one who is not capable of it, the most complete statements needed are the significations contained in the precious Book.

(10) What this man [al-Ghazālī] said in contending against them is good. And in contending against them, the soul should by all means be posited as immortal—as is signified by the intellectual and the Law-based indications. And it should be posited that what comes back [to life] are bodies like these which were in this abode—not these very ones, because what has perished does not come back as an individual entity. Existence comes back only to a likeness of what has perished, not to what has itself perished, as Abū Ḥāmid [al-Ghazālī] has explained. Therefore, the statement about coming back in the doctrine of the dialectical theologians, who believe that the soul is an accident and that the bodies that come back are those that have perished, is not correct. That is because what perishes, then exists, is one in kind—not one in number. Rather, it is two in number. And [it is not correct] in particular for those of them who say that accidents do not last during two periods of time.

[IV. Conclusion]

(11) This man [al-Ghazālī] accuses the philosophers of unbelief with respect to three questions. One of them is this one, and we have said enough about the opinion of the philosophers with respect to this question and that, according to them, it is one of the theoretical questions. The second question is their saying that He does not know particulars, and we have also said that this is not a statement of theirs. The third is their statement about the eternity of the world, and we have also said that what they mean by this name is not the meaning for which they are accused of unbelief by the dialectical theologians. In this book [*The Incoherence of the Philosophers*], he said that not a single Muslim speaks about spiritual return. Yet in others, he says that the Sufis do speak about it and that, accordingly, there is no consensus for accusing of unbelief those who speak about spiritual but not about sense-perceptible return and that speaking about spiritual return is permitted. In yet another book, moreover, he repeats this accusation of unbelief based on consensus. So, as you see, all of this is confused. God is the one who conduces to what is correct and selects whom He wills for the truth.

(12) I came to the opinion I would stop speaking about these things here and would ask to be pardoned for discussing them. Were it not for the necessity of seeking the truth with the one capable of it—and he, as Galen says, is one in a thousand—and resisting discussing it with those not capable of it, I would not have discussed that. God knows every letter, and perhaps God will accept my asking for pardon about that and excuse my stumbling through His grace, nobility, goodness, and superiority. There is no Lord but He!

Notes

Note to the Biographical Sketch of Averroës

1. ʿAbd al-Muʾmin ruled from 1128 until his death in 1163. His eldest son, Muḥammad, who had been named his successor, was such a profligate that he was able to rule only forty-five days before being deposed. The brother next in line, ʿUmar, willingly stepped aside and allowed the next brother, Abū Yaʿqūb Yūsuf, to succeed because he discerned so clearly Abū Yaʿqūb's merits.

Notes to the Translator's Introduction
of the *Decisive Treatise*

1. See Harvey C. Mansfield, Jr., "Strauss's Machiavelli," *Political Theory* 3, no. 4 (November 1975): 372–84; see 372.

2. See Muhsin S. Mahdi, "Remarks on Averroes' *Decisive Treatise*," in *Islamic Theology and Philosophy: Studies in Honor of George F. Hourani*, ed. Michael E. Marmura (Albany, N.Y.: SUNY Press, 1984): 188–202, 305–8; and "Averroës on Divine Law and Human Wisdom," in *Ancients and Moderns: Essays on the Tradition of Political Philosophy in Honor of Leo Strauss*, ed. Joseph Cropsey (New York: Basic Books, 1964), 114–31.

3. See four works by Léon Gauthier: *La théorie d'Ibn Rochd (Averroès) sur les rapports de la religion et de la philosophie* (Paris: Vrin, 1908); "Scolastique musulmane et scolastique chrétienne: À propos d'un livre récent," *Revue d'histoire de la philosophie* 2, no. 3 (1928): 221–53; no. 4 (1928), 333–65; *Averroès, Traité décisif* (Façl al-maqāl) *sur l'accord de la religion et de la philosophie, suivi de l'appendice* (Dhamīma) (Algiers: Éditions Carbonel, 1942); and *Ibn Rochd (Averroès)* (Paris: Presses Universitaires de France, 1948). See also *The Philosophy and Theology of Averroes*, trans. Muhammad Jamil al-Rahman (Baroda: A.G. Widgery, 1921); *Averroes on the Harmony of Religion and Philosophy: A Translation, with Introduction and Notes, of Ibn Rushd's* Kitāb faṣl al-maqāl, *with Its Appendix* (Ḍamīma) *and an Extract from* Kitāb al-kashf ʿan manāhij al-adilla, trans. George F. Hourani (London: Luzac, 1976); *Faṣl al-maqāl, fī mā bayn al-ḥikma wa al-sharīʿa min al-ittiṣāl, dirāsa wa taḥqīq*, ed. Muḥammad ʿAmāra (Cairo: Dār al-Maʿārif, 1969; 2d ed., 1983); *Averroè: Il trattato decisivo, sull'accordo della religione con la filosofia,*

trans. Massimo Campanini (Milan: Biblioteca Universale Rizzoli, 1994); *L'accordo della legge divina con la filosofia: Averroè,* trans. Francesca Lucchetta (Genoa: Marietti, 1994); *Averroès: Le livre du discours décisif,* trans. Marc Geoffroy, intro. Alain de Libera (Paris: Flammarion, 1996); *Faṣl al-maqāl, fī taqrīr mā bayn al-sharīʿa wa al-ḥikma min al-ittiṣāl aw wujūb al-naẓar al-ʿaqlī wa ḥudūd al-taʾwīl (al-dīn wa al-mujtamaʿ),* ed. Muḥammad ʿĀbid al-Jābirī, text established by Muḥammad ʿAbd al-Wāḥid al-ʿAsarī (Beirut: Markaz Dirāsāt al-Waḥdat al-ʿArabiyya, 1997); *Two Andalusian Philosophers: The Story of Hayy Ibn Yaqzan and the Definitive Statement,* trans. Jim Colville (London: Kegan Paul International, 1999).

In *Averroes on the Harmony,* 18 n. 6, Hourani gives bibliographical details concerning related studies by Miguel Asín Palacios, Manuel Alonso, and Michel Allard, as well as of Max Horten's translation of the *Decisive Treatise* and A. Bonucci's review of it. To these should be added the article by Jacques Langhade and Dominique Mallet, "Droit et philosophie au XIIe siècle dans al-Andalus: Averroès (Ibn Rushd)," *Revue de l'Occident musulman et de la Méditérranée* (numéro spécial, al-Andalus), no. 40 (1985): 103–21.

4. The section references are to the English translation of the text presented herein. The numbers in brackets are page and line references to Marcus Joseph Müller's original Arabic edition, *Philosophie und Theologie von Averroes* (Munich: n.p., 1859).

5. Mahdi speaks of these sections and subsections obliquely, for he is intent upon pointing to particular features of the work's teaching. From what he does say, he seems to have the following schema in mind (letters denote the five sections and lowercase roman numerals the seventeen subsections):

A.   Introduction (§1 [1.1–9]) plus philosophy and the Law
       (§2 [1.10–2.8])
   i.   Philosophy and the Law (§2 [1.10–2.8])
B.   The Law and syllogistic reasoning (§§3–4 [2.9–3.12])
   ii. Obligation to reflect upon existing things (§3 [2.9–12])
   iii. Obligation to learn about logic and its parts (§4 [2.13–3.12])
C.   How to acquire knowledge of syllogistic reasoning
       (§§5–10 [3.13–6.14])
   iv. Obligation to study syllogistic reasoning or invent it
         (§5 [3.13–19])
   v.   Obligation to use predecessors, if they exist (§6 [3.20–4.2])
   vi. Obligation to use the books of the Ancients (§7 [4.3–6])
   vii. Obligation to use demonstration to study existing things
         (§8 [4.7–5.7])
   viii. Obligation to use the books of foreign predecessors
         (§§9–10 [5.8–6.14])
D.   How the community of Muslims assents to the teachings
       of the Law (§§11–28 [6.14–15.21])
   ix. Three ways to communicate the Law (§11 [6.14–7.6])
   x.   Demonstration does not conflict with the Law (§12 [7.7–9])
   xi. If conflict, then interpretation (§13 [7.10–18])
   xii. Parallel with jurist (§§14–15 [7.19–9.17])
   xiii. Limits of consensus (§16 [9.18–10.16])

xiv. Human and divine knowledge (§§17–25 [10.17–14.17])

xv. All must assent to the roots of the Law (§§26–28 [14.18–15.21])

E. Interpretation and the Law (§§29–37 [15.21–18.19])

xvi. Apparent sense of the Law admits no interpretation (§§29–31 [15.21–16.19])

xvii. On the next life (§§32–37 [16.20–18.19])

6. The Madrid Biblioteca Nacional manuscript has no title; see Hourani, Arabic text, n. A.

7. Averroës insists at §10 [5.13] that the "aim and intention" of the Ancients "in their books is the very intention to which the Law urges us."

8. Thus, I understand the text to be divided as follows:

A. Introduction (§1 [1.1–9])

B. Philosophy and logic are obligatory (§§2–10 [1.10–6.14])

C. Demonstration and the Law accord (§§11–36 [6.14–18.14])

D. Summary (§37 [18.14–19])

E. The Law's intent and methods (§§38–51 [18.19–23.18])

F. On factions within Islam (§§52–58 [23.19–25.19])

G. Conclusion (§§59–60 [25.20–26.14])

Subparts B–D correspond to Mahdi's "part one" and subparts E–G to his "part two." As will become apparent from the ensuing discussion, subparts B and F seem to admit of further division into two smaller segments each and subparts C and E into three each. Some of those smaller segments also admit of division—but more on that in its proper place.

9. This is the first objection. Like that at §15 [8.15–17] (concerning whether demonstration can contravene consensus with respect to the interpretation of verses), it is indirect. The other three are all phrased as though meant to challenge Averroës directly: §16 [9.18–20], asking for a response to the charges brought by al-Ghazālī against al-Fārābī and Avicenna; §32 [16.20–21], inquiring into which of the three ranks of the Law he would place the verses concerning the hereafter; and §55 [24.14–17], seeking for "the shared methods by which the Lawgiver intended to teach the multitude."

10. See also Mahdi, "Remarks," 199–200 and n. 16. As Mahdi notes, this same softening of the conclusion occurs three other times in the immediate sequel: §7 [4.5], §8 [4.9–10], and §9 [5.7–8]. Note that in the translation (§4 [2:20]), the phrase is rendered: "therefore, . . . one . . . perhaps comes under the obligation . . ."

11. See §4 [3.5–7]; similar comparisons occur at §14 [7.19–20], §23 [14.2], and §24 [14.10–12].

12. But while adducing an additional argument here, Averroës also suppresses one. Insisting that "reflection upon intellectual syllogistic reasoning" must be believed to be as obligatory as "reflection upon juridical syllogistic reasoning and its kinds," he notes elliptically, "for this there is a reason, but this is not the place to mention it" (§4 [3.10]).

13. The argument occurs in al-Kindī's *Al-falsafa al-ūlā* (First philosophy); see *Rasāʾil al-Kindī al-falsafiyya* (Al-Kindī's philosophical epistles), ed. M. A. Abū Rīda, 2d ed. (Cairo: Maṭbaʿat Ḥassān, 1978), vol. 1, 33.11–13: "We ought not to be ashamed of appreciating the truth and acquiring it from wherever it comes, even if it comes from races remote from us and nations distinct [from

us]; for there is nothing more worthy than the truth for anyone who seeks the truth" (my translation). See also vol. 1, 32.13–33.9.

14. See above, n. 10.

15. There are only two exceptions to the power of the Law to reach all people: individual recalcitrance and inattentiveness. Nothing set forth here by Averroës seeks to deny freedom of choice. All that can be done is to acknowledge that some people refuse to believe and, thus, that the tools brought—perhaps even used—by the Prophet have limits. See §26 [15.3–8].

16. See §§23–24 [13.17–14.12], §§25–26 [14.13–15.8], and §27 [15.9–16], respectively.

17. Consider the example offered in §28 [15.19–21], and see also Averroës, *Tahāfut al-tahāfut* (Incoherence of the Incoherence), ed. Maurice Bouyges (Beirut: Imprimerie Catholique, 1930), 580.1–588.6. For a translation of this passage, see the appendix.

18. Al-Ghazālī's disarming candor in the last chapter of *Mīzān al-ʿamal* (The scale of labor) about how little importance he attaches to particular doctrines may have prompted part of the criticism Averroës levels against him here. See *Mīzān al-ʿamal* (Cairo: Maktaba wa Maṭbaʿa Muḥammad ʿAlī Ṣubiḥ wa Awlādihi, 1963), 124–26.

19. See §10 [5.13] and §28 [15.19–21] for earlier instances of intention discussed with respect to the Law. When intention is mentioned at §14 [8.2–4], it has nothing to do with the Law. Though "intention" and words derived from it occur only six times in this part of the *Decisive Treatise*, they occur fifteen times in the next. Fully ten refer to the Law or Lawgiver. See §38 [18.20], §39 [19.10 and 15], §40 [19.20–21], §48 [22.8 (twice)], §54 [24.13], §55 [24.15], §56 [25.1], and §59 [25.20]. The other five do not: §41 [20.5, 10, and 14] and §48 [22.8 and 9].

20. For other instances of Averroës speaking to the addressee in such a direct manner, see §15 [8.20–21] (on consensus with respect to theoretical matters), §16 [9.18] (an objection raised by the addressee about the teachings of al-Fārābī and Avicenna), §29 [15.21] (summarizing the preceding discussion of what verses can be interpreted), §48 [22.16–17] (drawing a conclusion from the comparison of the physician and the Lawgiver), and §51 [23.15] (a summary statement about the limits on interpretation).

21. See §50 [23.7–14].

22. The emphasis in this whole subpart on the more numerous among the believers—the multitude *(al-jumhūr)*—and their needs, as distinct from the select few *(al-khawāṣṣ)*, is worth noting. Indeed, the term "multitude" occurs fourteen times here and five times in the next subpart: §41 [20.14], §42 [20.17], §43 [20.20 and 21.2], §44 [21.5 and 9], §45 [21.14], §46 [21.20], §47 [22.6 (twice) and 7], §49 [23.2], §51 [23.16], §52 [23.21], §53 [24.2 and 3], §55 [24.15 and 20], and §60 [26.12]. On the other hand, the term "select" occurs only about a third as frequently—three times each in this subpart and the next, and once in the final subpart: §40 [19.21], §41 [20.14], §42 [20.16], §53 [24.2 and 3], §55 [24.19], and §60 [26.14].

23. The verse was first cited at §14 [8.13–14] and then again at §16 [10.6–10]. Its punctuation is not discussed in §14, and only in §16 does Averroës urge placing the stop after "and those well grounded in science." The goal

there is not to identify the particular verses that may be interpreted, nor to offer plausible interpretations, but merely to insist that some verses—agreed by all to admit of interpretation—should be explained to, or interpreted by, only "those well grounded in science."

24. And also, perhaps, to inculpate an unidentified group of pseudophilosophers; see Hourani, *Averroes on the Harmony,* nn. 172 and 195.

25. The full phrase warrants consideration: "It is obligatory for whoever wants to remove this heretical innovation from the Law to apply himself to the precious Book and pick from it the indications existing for every single thing we are responsible for believing" (§57 [25.6–8]).

26. For a succinct account of the stages of the debate as they affect the interpretation of Averroës' *Decisive Treatise,* see Mahdi, "Averroës on Divine Law," 114–17.

Note to the Translator's Introduction of the *Epistle Dedicatory*

1. See Muhsin Mahdi, "Averroës on Divine Law," 118 and also 117–23. According to Mahdi, Léon Gauthier hesitated momentarily about the proper appellation for this little treatise; see ibid., n. 17, and Gauthier, *Traité décisif,* vi and 49.

Notes to the Translation of the *Decisive Treatise*

1. Unless otherwise indicated, the term translated throughout this treatise as "Law" is *sharīʿa* or its equivalent, *sharʿ*. In this treatise, the terms are used to refer only to the revealed law of Islam. Elsewhere, however, Averroës uses the term *sharīʿa* to refer to revealed law generally. Because the term "legal" may be misleading for modern readers, even when capitalized and rendered "Legal," the adjectival form of *sharīʿa*—that is, *sharʿi*—is rendered here as "Law-based."

In his justly famous manual of law, Averroës explains that the jurists acknowledge the judgments of the divine Law to fall into five categories: obligatory *(wājib)*, recommended *(mandūb)*, prohibited *(maḥzūr)*, reprehensible *(makrūh)*, and permitted *(mubāḥ)*. Here, however, he groups the first two under a more comprehensive category of "commanded" *(maʾmūr)* and—perhaps since it is not applicable to the present question—passes over "reprehensible" in silence. See *Bidāyat al-mujtahid wa nihāyat al-muqtaṣid,* ed. ʿAbd al-Ḥalīm Muḥammad ʿAbd al-Ḥalīm and ʿAbd al-Raḥmān Ḥasan Maḥmūd (Cairo: Dār al-Kutub al-Ḥadītha, 1975), vol. 1, 17–18. The alliterative title, pointing to the work's character as a primer on Islamic Law, can be rendered in English as *The Legal Interpreter's Beginning and the Mediator's Ending.*

2. *Maʿrifa:* Similarly, *ʿarafa* is translated as "to be cognizant" and *ʿārif* as "cognizant" or "one who is cognizant." *ʿIlm,* on the other hand, is translated as "knowledge" or "science," *ʿalima* as "to know," and *ʿālim* as "knower" or "learned." It is important to preserve the distinctions between the Arabic terms in English—distinctions that seem to reflect those between *gignōskein* and *epistasthai* in Greek—because Averroës goes on to speak of human

cognizance of God as well as of God's knowledge of particulars (see below, §§4, 17).

3. In this treatise, Averroës uses the terms "book of God" and "precious Book" to indicate the Qurʾān. The numbers within brackets refer to chapters and verses of the Qurʾān. All translations from the Qurʾān are my own.

4. Normally the term *qiyās* is translated as "syllogism," this being an abridgment of "syllogistic reasoning." Here and in what follows, I translate it as "syllogistic reasoning" in order to bring out the way Averroës seems to be using the term.

5. The rest of the verse reads, ". . . one of those who have certainty."

6. *Al-muʾmin:* Throughout this treatise, *amana* is translated as "to have faith" and *imān* as "faith," while *iʿtaqada* is translated as "to believe," *muʿtaqid* as "believer," and *iʿtiqād* as "belief."

7. *Al-mutaqaddim:* Comes from the same verb that has been translated heretofore as "set out"—namely, *taqaddama.*

8. Actually, if the diameter of the earth is used as the unit of measure, it is about 109 times greater.

9. *Munāẓara:* Has the same root as *naẓar,* translated throughout this treatise as "reflection."

10. That is, the western part of the Islamic world—North Africa and Spain.

11. As is evident from the subtitle of the treatise, *ḥikma* (wisdom) is used interchangeably with *falsafa* to mean "philosophy." Nonetheless, the original difference between the two is respected here in that *ḥikma* is always translated as "wisdom" and *falsafa* as "philosophy."

12. That is, the books of the Ancients referred to above.

13. The reference is to the Qurʾān 16:69 where, speaking of bees, it is said, "There comes forth from their innards a drink of variegated colors in which there is healing for mankind."

14. That is, to all human beings—the red (or white) and the black.

15. *Ikhrāj dalālat al-lafẓ min al-dalāla al-ḥaqīqiyya ilā al-dalāla al-mujāziyya:* The language here is somewhat ambiguous and reads, literally, "drawing the significance of an utterance out from its true significance to its figurative significance." Heretofore, the term *dalāla* has been translated as "indication."

16. *Ajmaʿa:* From it is derived the noun "consensus" (*ijmāʿ*). Consensus is accepted in some schools of Islamic Law as a root or source of Law after the Qurʾān and Tradition (*ḥadīth*). Its validity as a root of the Law comes from a Tradition that reports the Prophet to have declared, "Indeed, God would not let my nation form a consensus about an error."

17. Those who follow the theological teachings of Abū al-Ḥasan ʿAli al-Ashʿarī (260/873–324/935). He was a pupil of the Muʿtazilites (see below, §43 and n. 44). When two sets of dates are given and are separated by a slash mark, as here, the first set refers to the dates of the *Anno Hejirae* (that is, the Islamic calendar that starts with the Prophet's flight to Medina) and the second set to the common era.

18. The verse reads, "He it is who created for you everything that is in the earth; then He directed Himself up toward the heavens, and He made them congruous as seven heavens; He is knowledgeable about everything." The Tradition in question is, "God descends to the lower world."

19. Those who follow the teachings of Aḥmad ibn Ḥanbal (164/780–241/855). A strict literalist, he was opposed to the Muᶜtazilites.

20. The whole verse reads: "He it is who has sent down to you the Book; in it, there are fixed verses—these being the mother of the Book—and others that resemble one another. Those with deviousness in their hearts pursue the ones that resemble one another, seeking discord and seeking to interpret them. None knows their interpretation but God and those well grounded in science. They say, 'We believe in it; everything is from our Lord.' And none heeds but those who are mindful."

The distinction between the "fixed verses" *(āyāt muḥkamāt)* and those that "resemble one another" *(mutashābihāt)* is that the former admit of no interpretation, whereas the latter are somewhat ambiguous or open-ended and do admit of interpretation—the question being, interpretation to what end? As will become evident in the sequel, there is some question as to where the clause explaining who "knows their interpretation" ends. Some hold that it ends after "God," so that the remainder of the verse reads, "And those well grounded in science say, 'We believe in it. . . .' " Others, like Averroës, hold that it reads as presented here. See below, §16.

21. Abū Ḥāmid al-Ghazālī (450/1058–505/1111) was a famous theologian who, as Averroës observes below, attacked the philosophers. In *Fayṣal al-tafriqa* (Arbitrator of the distinction), al-Ghazālī explains the limits to be placed on charging others with unbelief and notes in particular that going against consensus is not to be considered unbelief. He gives two reasons for this: first, consensus usually concerns the branches of faith rather than the roots; second, it is very difficult to determine what there is consensus about. The roots of faith are three, according to al-Ghazālī: faith in God, in his messenger, and in the hereafter. See *Al-quṣūr al-ᶜawālī min rasāʾil al-Imām al-Ghazālī* (Cairo: al-Jundī, n.d.), 161–68, especially 165–66.

Abū al-Maᶜālī al-Juwaynī (419/1028–478/1085), who is also known as Imām al-Ḥaramayn, was an Ashᶜarite theologian and also al-Ghazālī's teacher.

22. *Aʾimmat al-naẓar:* Literally, "leaders of reflection."

23. *Al-naẓariyyāt:* Literally, "reflective matters." Unless otherwise noted, all future occurrences of the term "theoretical" are to translate this adjectival sense of *naẓar.*

24. A transmission is deemed to be uninterrupted when we know that one person has related the particular doctrine to another through the ages so that it comes down to us with no break in the chain of authorities attesting to its authenticity. This is one of the criteria for judging the soundness of Traditions about the Prophet; see the next note.

25. Muḥammad ibn Ismāᶜil al-Bukhārī (194/810–256/870) is the author of one of the six canonical collections of Tradition—that is, accounts of things the Prophet and his companions said and did. ᶜAlī ibn Abū Ṭālib (d. 41/661) was the fourth orthodox caliph.

26. The charge is brought by al-Ghazālī at the very end of his book, but he deftly sidesteps the question associated with it of whether those who accept such beliefs are to be put to death; see *Tahāfut al-falāsifa,* ed. Maurice Bouyges (Beirut: Imprimerie Catholique, 1927), 376.2–10; also 21–94, 223–38, and

344–37. In addition to attempting to defend the philosophers here, Averroës wrote a detailed refutation of al-Ghazālī's charges in the *Tahāfut al-tahāfut,* ed. Maurice Bouyges (Beirut: Imprimerie Catholique, 1930), 4–117, 455–68, and 580–86; see also 587. The English translation by Simon Van Den Bergh, *Averroes' Tahafut al-Tahafut (The Incoherence of the* Incoherence*)* (Oxford: Oxford University Press, 1954), has Bouyges's page numbers in the margins. Abū Naṣr al-Fārābī was born in 257/870 and died in 339/950; Abū ᶜAlī al-Ḥusayn ibn Sīnā, or Avicenna, was born in 370/980 and died in 428/1037.

27. See *Fayṣal al-tafriqa*, 168–71. Averroës thus reads this subsequent passage as modifying the earlier assertion (pp. 163–64) that the philosophers are to be charged with unbelief for what they say about God's knowledge of particulars and their denial of the resurrection of bodies and punishments in the next life.

28. See above, §14 and n. 20.

29. That is, the verses of the Qurᵓān; and this becomes clear in what follows.

30. In his *Middle Commentary on Aristotle's* Categories, Averroës explains Aristotle's account of homonymous names as follows:

> He said: things having homonymous—that is, shared—names are things which have not a single thing in common and shared, except for the name alone. The definition of each one which makes its substance understood according to the way it is denoted by that shared name is different from the definition of the other one and is particular to what it defines. An example of that is the name "animal" said of a depicted man and of a rational man.

See *Averroës' Middle Commentaries on Aristotle's* Categories *and* De Interpretatione, trans. Charles E. Butterworth (South Bend, Ind.: St. Augustine's Press, 1998), section 3, from which the above translation comes. The term "shared" can also be understood as "ambiguous"; see sections 57–58.

Though *al-jalal* is usually used to speak of something that is momentous or magnificent, it can also be used to signify what is paltry or petty. The basic sense of *al-ṣarīm* is that of cutting; thus, it is used to speak both of daybreak or dawn as though cut off from the night and of night as though cut off from the day. See E. W. Lane, *An Arabic-English Lexicon* (1877; reprint, London: Islamic Texts Society, 1984), 1684 col. 3.

31. Namely, the *Epistle Dedicatory.* For an explanation of the title of this work and of its subtitle, *The Question the Shaykh Abū al-Walīd Mentioned in the* Decisive Treatise, as well as of its place with respect to the *Decisive Treatise* and the third part of the trilogy—the *Kashf ᶜan manāhij al-adilla fī ᶜaqāᵓid al-milla* (Uncovering the methods of proofs with respect to the beliefs of the religious community)—see the introduction to the *Epistle Dedicatory.*

32. *Sabab fāᶜil:* Unless otherwise noted, *sabab* is always translated as "reason" in this treatise. However, to render the term *sabab fāᶜil* as "reason agent" here would make no sense.

33. The term is *fāᶜil* and, were it not for the declaration at the end of the next paragraph, might better be rendered here as "Maker."

34. That is, the Traditions concerning what the Prophet said and did *(al-sunna)*; see above, n. 25. This is one of the roots or sources of the divine Law, along with the Qurᵓān and consensus.

35. *Ijtihād:* Refers to personal judgment about an interpretation of the Law.

36. *Asbāb*, sing. *sabab:* See n. 32 above.

37. Existing things are identified by al-Ghazālī as: *dhātī* (essential), *ḥissī* (sense-perceptible), *khiyālī* (imaginary), *ʿaqlī* (intelligible), and *shibhī* (figurative); see *Fayṣal al-tafriqa*, 150–56. Though al-Ghazālī definitely enumerates these five sorts or ranks of existing things and explains them with respect to interpretations, Averroës' uncertainty here about how many sorts or kinds al-Ghazālī actually enumerated implies that the account is not obvious. He may be referring to the way al-Ghazālī excludes the first rank—essential—from being interpreted or, alternatively, to the way al-Ghazālī brings together the sense-perceptible and imaginary ranks.

38. See above, §14 and n. 18.

39. See above, §§14 and 16 and nn. 20 and 28.

40. *Tanbīh al-fiṭar:* Literally, "alert the innate dispositions."

41. The verse is by ʿImrān ibn Ḥiṭṭān al-Sadūsī, a poet who lived in the seventh century. South Arabian tribes were considered to be Yamanites, whereas north Arabian tribes—among them the Maʿaddī—were considered to be Adnānites.

42. The verse is part of Luqmān's instruction to his son by way of preaching and reads in full, "And thus Luqmān said to his son, while preaching to him, 'Oh, son, do not associate [other gods] with God, for associating [other gods with God] is surely a major wrong.'" Averroës uses it to illustrate how great the injustice or wrong can become when the learned, prohibited from reading demonstrative books, are led to ignorance of the greatest of all beings, God, and thus to polytheism.

43. That is, in accordance with the preceding section, limited to fewer people.

44. The Muʿtazilites constituted the first school of dialectical theology in the Islamic tradition. They enjoyed the support of the Abbasid caliphs during the middle part of the ninth century but were attacked by the Ashʿarites.

45. *Kamā ṣanaʿa dhālika Abū Ḥāmid:* Or, in keeping with the way Averroës has used this verb heretofore, "as Abū Ḥāmid [al-Ghazālī] artfully did."

46. See above, § 14 and n. 20. The verses that "resemble one another" are thus ambiguous and difficult to explain, at times so difficult that it seems "none knows their interpretation but God."

47. Literally, "statements of shared assent" *(aqāwīl mushtarikat al-taṣdīq);* see below, §§53–55 and 57.

48. The context is animal sacrifice. Neither the flesh nor the blood of camels will affect God, but human piety will.

49. The rest of the verse reads ". . . but they refused to bear it and shirked it, whereas mankind bore it. Indeed, he was unjust and ignorant."

50. *Al-musabbabāt:* Plural past participle of *sabab*, "reason."

51. The three methods consist of two that are shared by the majority of people (namely, the rhetorical and the dialectical) and one limited to the select few (the demonstrative); see above, §§40, 44, and 53–54.

52. The reference is to the rule of the Almohade sovereign, Abū Yaʿqūb Yūsuf (reigned 1163–1184).

Notes to the Translation of the *Epistle Dedicatory*

1. That is, the knowledge possessed by the eternal being, or God; hence the capitalization. Throughout the argument, divine or eternal knowledge is contrasted with human or generated knowledge.

2. The term is *ʿadam*, which is usually translated as "privation." Given the context, however, it seems more appropriate to translate it and its derivatives (for example, *maʿdūm*), here and in what follows, as "nonexistence" or "nonexisting."

3. See al-Ghazālī, *Tahāfut al-falāsifa*, Thirteenth Question, 223–34, esp. 229.4–234.4; and Averroës, *Tahāfut al-tahāfut*, 455–63, esp. 458.5–460.14 and 460.15–463.15.

4. *Al-ghāʾib:* Literally, "what is absent."

5. The term translated as "wrongness" is *fasād* and thus could be rendered as "corruption." The verb translated as "recognized" is *ʿurifa*; see above, *Decisive Treatise*, n. 2.

6. The text has the plural (*ilhāmāt*, sing. *ilhām*).

Notes to the Appendix

1. From Averroës, *Tahāfut al-Tahāfut* (Incoherence of the Incoherence), ed. Maurice Bouyges (Beirut: Imprimerie Catholique, 1930), 580.1–580.6. The translation is my own, and I am also responsible for dividing the text into sections and paragraphs.

2. The immediate antecedent of the feminine singular pronoun (*hā*), which may be used to refer to inanimate plural things, must be "Laws" (*sharāʾiʿ*). In the context, it must be understood as the Laws establishing the resurrection of bodies.

3. Here and in the rest of the passage until the end of this paragraph, the pronoun "they" refers to the Laws.

4. That is, someone who is of the select sort. Averroës moves here from speaking about the group and what its individual members do as members of the group to speaking about the individual within the group.

5. The immediate and most likely antecedent of the feminine singular pronoun (*hā*) is "religion" (*milla*). As the preceding paragraph suggests, each religion is based on a particular Law.

6. *Wujūb al-ʿamal:* Literally, "what practice makes obligatory," or even "the obligation of practice."

7. Reading *al-ṣalwa*, with the Istanbul Yeni Jāmiʿ manuscript no. 734, to accord with the verse from the Qurʾān, rather than *al-ṣalawāt*, with Bouyges, on the basis of the other manuscripts. See *Decisive Treatise*, §50.

8. The rest of the verse reads, ". . . and partaking of it and of its shade is perpetual. That is the outcome of those who are pious, and the outcome of the unbelievers is the fire."

Bibliography

Averroës. *Averroè: Il trattato decisivo, sull'accordo della religione con la filosofia.* Trans. Massimo Campanini. Milan: Biblioteca Universale Rizzoli, 1994.

———. *Averroès: Le livre du discours décisif.* Trans. Marc Geoffroy. Intro. Alain de Libera. Paris: Flammarion, 1996.

———. *Averroes' Middle Commentaries on Aristotle's* Categories *and* De Interpretatione. Trans. Charles E. Butterworth. 1983. Reprint, South Bend, Ind.: St. Augustine's Press, 1998.

———. *Averroes on the Harmony of Religion and Philosophy: A Translation, with Introduction and Notes, of Ibn Rushd's* Kitāb faṣl al-maqāl, *with Its Appendix* (Damīma) *and an Extract from* Kitāb al-kashf ʿan manāhij al-adilla. Trans. George F. Hourani. London: Luzac, 1976.

———. *Averroes' Tahafut al-Tahafut (The Incoherence of the* Incoherence*).* Trans. Simon Van Den Bergh. Oxford: Oxford University Press, 1954.

———. *Averroès, Traité décisif* (Façl al-maqāl) *sur l'accord de la religion et de la philosophie, suivi de l'appendice* (Dhamīma). Trans. Léon Gauthier. Algiers: Éditions Carbonel, 1942.

———. *Bidāyat al-mujtahid wa nihāyat al-muqtaṣid.* Ed. ʿAbd al-Ḥalīm Muḥammad ʿAbd al-Ḥalīm and ʿAbd al-Raḥmān Ḥasan Maḥmūd. 2 vols. Cairo: Dār al-Kutub al-Ḥadītha, 1975.

———. *Faṣl al-maqāl, fī mā bayn al-ḥikma wa al-sharīʿa min al-ittiṣāl, dirāsa wa taḥqīq.* Ed. Muḥammad ʿAmāra. Cairo: Dār al-Maʿārif, 1969. 2d ed., 1983.

———. *Faṣl al-maqāl, fī taqrīr mā bayn al-sharīʿa wa al-ḥikma min al-ittiṣāl aw wujūb al-naẓar al-ʿaqlī wa ḥudūd al-taʾwīl (al-dīn wa al-mujtamaʿ).* Ed. Muḥammad ʿĀbid al-Jābirī. Text established by Muḥammad ʿAbd al-Wāḥid al-ʿAsarī. Beirut: Markaz Dirāsāt al-Waḥdat al-ʿArabiyya, 1997.

———. *L'accordo della legge divina con la filosofia: Averroè.* Trans. Francesca Lucchetta. Genoa: Marietti, 1994.

———. *The Philosophy and Theology of Averroes.* Trans. Muhammad Jamil al-Rahman. Baroda: A. G. Widgery, 1921.

———. *Tahāfut al-tahāfut.* Ed. Maurice Bouyges. Bibliotheca Arabica Scholasticorum, série arabe, 3. Beirut: Imprimerie Catholique, 1930.

———. *Two Andalusian Philosophers: The Story of Hayy ibn Yaqzan and the Definitive Statement.* Trans. Jim Colville. London: Kegan Paul International, 1999.

Gauthier, Léon. *Ibn Rochd (Averroès)*. Paris: Presses Universitaires de France, 1948.

———. *La théorie d'Ibn Rochd (Averroès) sur les rapports de la religion et de la philosophie*. Paris: Vrin, 1908.

———. "Scolastique musulmane et scolastique chrétienne: À propos d'un livre récent." *Revue d'histoire de la philosophie* 2, no. 3 (1928): 221–53; 2, no. 4 (1928): 333–65.

al-Ghazālī, Abū Ḥāmid. *Fayṣal al-tafriqa*. In *Al-quṣūr al-ʿawālī min rasāʾil al-Imām al-Ghazālī*. Cairo: al-Jundī, n.d.

———. *Mīzān al-ʿamal*. Cairo: Maktaba wa Maṭbaʿa Muḥammad ʿAlī Ṣubīḥ wa Awlādihi, 1963.

———. *Tahāfut al-falāsifa*. Ed. Maurice Bouyges. Bibliotheca Arabica Scholasticorum, série arabe, 2. Beirut: Imprimerie Catholique, 1927.

al-Kindī. *Rasāʾil al-Kindī al-falsafiyya*. Ed. M. A. Abū Rīda. 2 vols. 2d ed. Cairo: Maṭbaʿat Ḥassān, 1978.

Lane, E. W. *An Arabic-English Lexicon*. 1877. Reprint, London: Islamic Texts Society, 1984.

Langhade, Jacques, and Dominique Mallet. "Droit et philosophie au XIIe siècle dans al-Andalus: Averroès (Ibn Rushd)." *Revue de l'Occident musulman et de la Méditérranée* (numéro spécial, al-Andalus), no. 40 (1985): 103–21.

Mahdi, Muhsin S. "Averroës on Divine Law and Human Wisdom." In *Ancients and Moderns: Essays on the Tradition of Political Philosophy in Honor of Leo Strauss*, ed. Joseph Cropsey, 114–31. New York: Basic Books, 1964.

———. "Remarks on Averroes' Decisive Treatise." In *Islamic Theology and Philosophy: Studies in Honor of George F. Hourani*, ed. Michael E. Marmura, 188–202, 305–8. Albany, N.Y.: SUNY Press, 1984.

Mansfield, Harvey C., Jr. "Strauss's Machiavelli." *Political Theory* 3, no. 3 (August 1975): 372–84.

Müller, Marcus Joseph. *Philosophie und Theologie von Averroes*. Munich: n.p., 1859.

Index of Qurʾānic Verses

Index of Names and Terms

About the Translator

CHARLES E. BUTTERWORTH, professor of government and politics at the University of Maryland, College Park, specializes in medieval Islamic political philosophy. After receiving his B.A. from Michigan State University, he studied political philosophy, Arabic, and Islamic civilization at the University of Chicago, earning an M.A. and Ph.D. in political science. He has also studied at the University of Ayn Shams in Egypt, the University of Bordeaux, and the University of Nancy, receiving from the latter a doctorate in philosophy. He has taught at numerous universities, including Chicago, Georgetown, and Harvard, as well as the Sorbonne, Bordeaux, Grenoble, and others in Belarus, Egypt, Germany, and Hungary. His publications include critical editions of most of Averroës' Middle Commentaries on Aristotle's logic; translations of works by Averroës, Al-Fārābī, Al-Rāzī, and Maimonides; and studies of the political teachings of these and other philosophical thinkers.

A Note on the Type

The English text of this book was set in BASKERVILLE, a typeface originally designed by John Baskerville (1706–1775), a British stonecutter, letter designer, typefounder, and printer. The Baskerville type is considered to be one of the first "transitional" faces—a deliberate move away from the "old style" of the Continental humanist printer. Its rounded letterforms presented a greater differentiation of thick and thin strokes, the serifs on the lower-case letters were more nearly horizontal, and the stress was nearer the vertical—all of which would later influence the "modern" style undertaken by Bodoni and Didot in the 1790s. Because of its high readability, particularly in long texts, the type was subsequently copied by all major typefoundries. (The original punches and matrices still survive today at Cambridge University Press.) This adaptation of Baskerville, designed by the Compugraphic Corporation in the 1960s, is a notable departure from other versions in its overall typographic evenness and lightness in color. To enhance its range, supplemental diacritics and ligatures were created in 1997 for exclusive use in the Islamic Translation Series.

TYPOGRAPHY BY JONATHAN SALTZMAN

◆